# INSTRUCTIONAL AGILITY

## Responding to *Assessment* With *Real-Time* Decisions

**CASSANDRA ERKENS** | **TOM SCHIMMER** | **NICOLE DIMICH VAGLE**

Solution Tree | Press *a division of* Solution Tree

the **Solution Tree** **Assessment Center**

555 North Morton Street

Bloomington, IN 47404

800.733.6786 (toll free) / 812.336.7700

FAX: 812.336.7790

email: info@SolutionTree.com

SolutionTree.com

Visit **go.SolutionTree.com/assessment** to download the free reproducibles in this book.

Printed in the United States of America

21   20   19   18   17       1   2   3   4   5

Library of Congress Cataloging-in-Publication Data

Names: Erkens, Cassandra, author. | Schimmer, Tom, author. | Dimich Vagle,
   Nicole, author.
Title: Instructional agility : responding to assessment with real-time
   decisions / Cassandra Erkens, Tom Schimmer, and Nicole Dimich Vagle.
Description: Bloomington, IN : Solution Tree Press, [2018] | Includes
   bibliographical references and index.
Identifiers: LCCN 2017022861 | ISBN 9781943874705 (perfect bound)
Subjects: LCSH: Teaching--Decision making. | Educational tests and
   measurements. | Individualized instruction. | Effective teaching. |
   Classroom management.
Classification: LCC LB1027 .E74 2018 | DDC 371.102--dc23 LC record available at https://lccn.loc.
gov/2017022861

**Solution Tree**

Jeffrey C. Jones, CEO
Edmund M. Ackerman, President

**Solution Tree Press**

*President and Publisher:* Douglas M. Rife
*Editorial Director:* Sarah Payne-Mills
*Art Director:* Rian Anderson
*Managing Production Editor:* Caroline Cascio
*Senior Production Editor:* Christine Hood
*Senior Editor:* Amy Rubenstein
*Copy Editor:* Miranda Addonizio
*Proofreader:* Elisabeth Abrams
*Text and Cover Designer:* Abigail Bowen
*Editorial Assistants:* Jessi Finn and Kendra Slayton

# ACKNOWLEDGMENTS

Solution Tree Press would like to thank the following reviewers:

Erin Balfour
English Teacher
McNeil High School
Austin, Texas

Paul Cancellieri
Science Teacher
Rolesville Middle School
Rolesville, North Carolina

Justin Kiel
Principal
McKinley Elementary School
Owatonna, Minnesota

Geraldine Lawlor
Principal
Mount Elizabeth Middle/Secondary
   School
Kitimat, British Columbia, Canada

Amber Teamann
Principal
Whitt Elementary School
Sachse, Texas

Visit **go.SolutionTree.com/assessment** to
download the free reproducibles in this book.

# TABLE OF CONTENTS

# 2 | *Engineering Engaging Conversations* . . . . . . . . **29**

# 3 | *Questioning.* . . . . . . . . . . . . . . . . . . . . **63**

# 6   *Practicing* . . . . . . . . . . . . . . . . . . . . . . . . . . . *123*

# 7   *Viewing Instructional Agility in the Broader Context* . . . . . . . . . . . . . . . . . . . . . *147*

# ABOUT THE AUTHORS

**Cassandra Erkens** is a presenter, facilitator, coach, trainer of trainers, keynote speaker, author, and above all, a teacher. She presents nationally and internationally on assessment, instruction, school improvement, and professional learning communities.

Cassandra has served as an adjunct faculty member at Hamline and Cardinal Stritch universities, where she took teachers through graduate education courses. She has authored and coauthored a wide array of published trainings, and she has designed and delivered the training of trainers programs for two major education-based companies.

As an educator and recognized leader, Cassandra has served as a senior high school English teacher, a director of staff development at the district level, a regional school improvement facilitator, and a director of staff and organization development in the private sector.

To learn more about Cassandra's work, visit http://allthingsassessment.info or follow @cerkens on Twitter.

**Tom Schimmer** is an author and a speaker with expertise in assessment, grading, leadership, and behavioral support. Tom is a former district-level leader, school administrator, and teacher. As a district-level leader, he was a member of the senior management team responsible for overseeing the efforts to support and build the instructional and assessment capacities of teachers and administrators.

Tom is a sought-after speaker who presents internationally for schools and districts. He has worked extensively throughout North America, as well as in Vietnam, Myanmar, China, Thailand, Japan, India, Qatar, Spain, and the United Arab Emirates. He earned a teaching degree from Boise State University and a master's degree in curriculum and instruction from the University of British Columbia.

To learn more about Tom's work, visit http://allthingsassessment.info or follow @TomSchimmer on Twitter.

 **Nicole Dimich Vagle** has a passion for education and lifelong learning, which has led her to extensively explore, facilitate, and implement innovative practices in school transformation. She works with elementary and secondary educators in presentations, trainings, and consultations that address today's most critical issues, all in the spirit of facilitating increased student learning and confidence.

Nicole was a school transformation specialist, where she coached individual teachers and teams of teachers in assessment, literacy, and high expectations for all students. Nicole was also a program evaluator and trainer at the Center for Supportive Schools in New Jersey. A former middle and high school English teacher, she is committed to making schools into places where all students feel invested and successful.

A featured presenter at conferences internationally, Nicole empowers educators to build their capacity for and implement engaging assessment design, formative assessment practices, common assessment design and analysis, response to intervention systems, data-driven decisions, student work protocols, and motivational strategies.

Nicole earned a master of arts degree in human development from Saint Mary's University and a bachelor of arts degree in English and psychology from Concordia College.

To learn more about Nicole's work, visit http://allthingsassessment.info or follow @NicoleVagle on Twitter.

To book Cassandra Erkens, Tom Schimmer, or Nicole Dimich Vagle for professional development, contact pd@SolutionTree.com.

# INTRODUCTION

*I was going to put my move to the test, to see if it was real. It had to be real if it worked on the greatest player to ever play the game.*

—Allen Iverson

On March 12, 1997, as future Hall of Fame basketball player Allen Iverson's rookie season in Philadelphia was drawing to a close, his 76ers were at home facing the reigning National Basketball Association champion Chicago Bulls. The Bulls were led by Michael Jordan, not just the best player in the league in 1997, but the player whom many considered to be the greatest basketball player of all time. Chicago would end the 1996–1997 season with sixty-nine wins and only thirteen losses, while Philadelphia would manage just twenty-two wins against sixty losses. The Bulls would go on to win not only the March 12 matchup 108–104 but also the 1996–1997 NBA championship.

However, for Iverson, the March 12 game was all about a *moment*, not who won or lost. During the second half of this closely fought game, Iverson would take a handoff on the left side of the court and dribble to the top of the three-point line; it was here he found himself one on one with none other than Michael Jordan. This was not the first time they had faced each other (this was their third meeting of the year), but this night was going to be different. Iverson would do something that few had ever done and that would cement his reputation as one of the most lethal offensive players in the NBA.

For those with little to no basketball acumen, here is some background on that moment, starting with a *crossover dribble*. The crossover dribble is effective because the offensive player makes no advanced decision to attack but simply *reacts* to what the defender does. In essence, the art of the crossover dribble is for the offensive player to make the defensive player *think* he or she is going in one direction, only to have him or her attack in the other. If the defensive player overcommits in one direction, the offensive player reacts, dribbles the ball to the opposite hand (crossover), and attacks the basket, trying to score or at least pass to another open teammate. The offensive player must, with some nimbleness, read the situation and immediately respond with quickness and agility; without the *agility* to adjust, the initial move (having the defender overcommit) is wasted since there will be time for the defender to recover.

The key is not just the ability to dribble the ball from one hand to the other—all NBA players can do that—but the ability to dribble with athletic *agility* and the ability *to read the situation* and *make a real-time decision* about when to pause, when to fake, and when to attack at maximum speed and intensity.

This athletic agility paid off during the game. When Iverson reached the top of the three-point line, he took two dribbles with his left hand, crossed to his right, sent the ball back through his legs to his left, dribbled once more on his left, and then attacked. Iverson dribble-faked to the left (Jordan moved with it), crossed to his right hand (Jordan recovered), paused, and then dribble-faked again to his left (this time Jordan overcommitted), crossed over back to his right (Jordan couldn't recover), pulled up from twenty feet and hit the jump shot!

Now, being the greatest of all time, Michael Jordan almost recovered to block the shot (which few could do), but he didn't. So, while Jordan was considered a smothering defender, Iverson was able to use his quickness and athletic agility to create the necessary space to hit the shot. Many pundits and former players still consider this moment to be the greatest crossover dribble in the history of the NBA.

# Instructional Agility

There are, of course, many differences between what happens on a basketball court and what happens in classrooms, but both environments require real-time decisions. When teachers use emerging evidence to make real-time decisions during instruction within the context of the learning they expect, they are demonstrating *instructional agility*. In many ways, teachers' best moves are tested every day against precise and exacting standards mixed with the social and political demands for the *growth* of all students toward proficiency. Limited time is the reality of all school systems. So, despite the fact that educators know learning is never final in the abstract, all school years come to an end. This means there is an inherent competition between students and the standards, not among students. Therefore, a teacher's ability to be instructionally agile on behalf of each student is critical to support his or her continual learning.

Whether at the classroom or school level, teachers can realize assessment's true power when emerging results determine what comes next in the learning. *Assessment* is the practice of gathering information about student learning; how educators use that information is what distinguishes formative from summative assessment. Teachers use assessment information formatively when it guides instructional decisions. At its most organic, intimate level, assessment information allows teachers to make those instructional decisions at a moment's notice; that's instructional agility.

Being athletically agile means one can move quickly and easily without interruption; being instructionally agile means essentially the same thing. Making quick yet thoughtful decisions about what comes next is the real power of assessment in the service of learning. Like basketball players, teachers know what they *want* to do but can't necessarily forge ahead without assessing the possibilities. Certainly teachers with experience, and those who have intentionally created activities that lend themselves to quick instructional transitions, can plan ahead for anticipated responses. Understanding the typical errors students make can assist in preplanning the potential paths forward, but there is always the chance of an unanticipated outcome. Willingness paired with readiness, and precision paired with flexibility, allow teachers to develop the nimbleness required to maximize the impact of instruction.

## Assessment and Standards-Based Learning

Since the late 1990s, education has seen an acceleration of research on formative assessment (Black, 2013) and the near unanimous conclusion that formative assessment and feedback are an essential part of improving student achievement (Ruiz-Primo & Li, 2013). While teachers have always used assessment to judge student performance, classroom assessment in the 2000s and beyond has seen an infusion of assessment *for* learning—assessment not used to judge, grade, or score, but assessment to identify what comes next.

The inertia of the standards movement throughout the 1990s brought about a renewed interest in formative assessment. As schools explored the most favorable courses of action for having students meet the identified standards, formative assessment emerged as the most effective and efficient manner through which to expedite learning. To be clear, the idea of formative assessment was not new; what was new was the impressive potential of formative assessment practices within the standards-based instructional paradigm.

Paul Black and Dylan Wiliam (1998) report that using assessment strategies to guide instruction through descriptive (rather than evaluative) feedback could bring about unrivaled achievement gains, with the lowest achievers benefitting the most. This pivotal moment accelerated the growth in formative assessment studies and produced an aligned position that when schools use assessment formatively, they can close the gap between where a student is and where the standards expect him or her to be (Chappuis, 2014; Heritage, 2010; Sadler, 1989). More than ever, educators now understand how they can carry out assessment during the instructional process to improve both teaching and learning (Shepard et al., 2005), and how it can create a more efficient, effective path to proficiency (Heritage, 2010; Popham, 2008).

Standards represent a clear vision or outcome for what students are to achieve at the end of the instructional experience, which means teachers can now create clearer pathways to proficiency. By *unpacking* standards (which means deconstructing standards by identifying the learning targets that form the instructional scaffolding necessary to achieve the entire standard), teachers create *learning progressions* that allow students to see, with much greater transparency, what it takes to reach expected performance levels. Of course, educators have always associated assessment with measurement, and certainly formative assessment is a kind of measurement. However, efforts to gather formative evidence lead educators to intentionally shift to *qualitative* assessment (descriptive information about misconceptions and next steps). This balances the already embedded *quantitative* purpose (numbers and data that represent certain levels of proficiency—these data often tell what and who, but not so much the why or what's next).

# Distracted by Data

Educators have, however, lost a little focus. While current assessment practices and tools demand a more sophisticated approach to classroom assessment, the shadow of the accountability movement has arguably diverted too much attention to quantifying every instructional moment. Teachers create formative assessment experiences that resemble a summative that "doesn't count." This happens when teachers use points on every assessment and make policies that make summative assessments worth more points and formative assessments worth fewer. Students perceive that those formative assessments, the important moments of practice, "don't count" because teachers simply don't add points in the gradebook. This distraction also occurs when every moment of assessment interrupts the learning progression. In other words, the teacher has to stop teaching in order to conduct a formative event. The impact of a teacher's instruction will not reach its full potential through a series of events that intentionally disconnect assessment from instruction. The first half of the formative assessment equation is timing these assessments within the instructional flow.

The second half of the formative assessment equation is quality feedback that identifies *what's next* for the student (Hattie, 2012). The research on effective feedback is rich, long-standing, and makes it clear that feedback in the absence of grades, scores, and levels is most impactful (Butler, 1988; Hattie & Timperley, 2007). In essence, grades and scores actually have the potential to neutralize the impact of educators' feedback because students either determine feedback to be unnecessary (when they achieve a satisfactory result) or undesirable or overwhelming (when they achieve an unsatisfactory result). Without a productive student response, feedback ceases to be effective (Kluger & DeNisi; 1996; Wiliam, 2011).

To be sure, data play an essential role in guiding a teacher's instructional decisions as well as determining the effectiveness of his or her instructional maneuvers and the overall general program when examined over time. The reference to data as a distraction is not a dismissal of the important process of tracking student learning. Individual classroom assessments, common assessments, interim benchmark assessments, and even large-scale assessments can provide data points useful for understanding the impact of instruction and can lead to maximizing the available instructional minutes. Data become a distraction when the accumulation of data—not the advancement of learning—is the motive behind planning the instructional activities. There is a place for data, but *real-time* teaching and learning are responsive to students in the moment, and teachers should not pause to update a spreadsheet.

## Assessment as a Verb

At its most organic, assessment is a *verb* we can infuse within the overall instructional process. Rather than having to stop teaching to conduct a formative assessment (noun), teachers move seamlessly among the moments of instruction, assessment, and feedback; though the lines still exist, they are blurry. The *assessment as noun* perspective leaves teachers with what appears to be an irreconcilable dilemma: *if I'm assessing my students day to day and minute by minute, when am I supposed to teach?* Seeing assessment as a noun—as a tangible event—creates the illusion that assessment is synonymous with a stapled package of questions and that assessment and instruction are two separate experiences.

The *assessment as verb* perspective allows teachers to assess and teach within a fluid instructional cycle where the teacher need not stop to conduct anything. Much like coaches, teachers can keep learning on track in real time and allow for the necessary maneuvers and advice to improve performance at a moment's notice. There is no moment when coaches are not assessing their athletes; they assess every serve, every tackle, every shot, and every rebound against the level of performance they desire (that is, the standard). In response, coaches provide immediate direction on how to close the gap between what the athlete displays and what they expect. Occasionally a coach will stop practice, however in most cases, he or she provides descriptive instructions *during* performance and expects the athlete to make the necessary adjustments on the fly. In other words, effective coaches are agile enough to know what needs to happen before the athletes' next opportunity to perform.

# Instructional Agility in Context

Instructional agility does not occur in a vacuum but rather in the context of sound assessment design and execution. In *Essential Assessment: Six Tenets for Bringing Hope, Efficacy, and Achievement to the Classroom* (Erkens, Schimmer, & Vagle, 2017), we outline a framework through which assessment practices can maximize both cognitive and affective outcomes for students. Instructional agility is one of these six tenets. Each tenet is contingent upon the other five, which means it is essential to understand how each of the other five tenets contributes to a teacher's ability to be instructionally agile. Figure I.1 outlines the assessment framework.

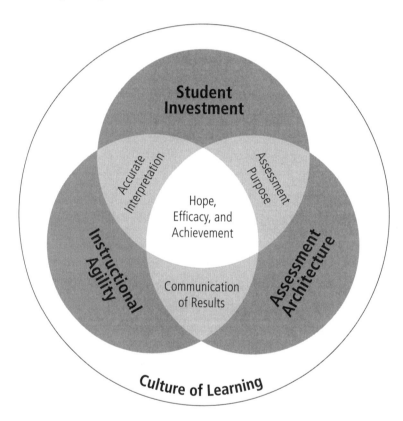

**Figure I.1: *The six assessment tenets framework.***
*Visit **go.SolutionTree.com/assessment** for a free reproducible version of this figure.*

At the center of all six tenets is the building of *hope*, *efficacy*, and *achievement*, which means students emerge from assessment experiences with increased achievement, an increased sense of efficacy, and an increased hopefulness for their potential success going forward. As well, the totality of any teacher's assessment systems should develop and nurture a culture of learning rather than accumulating points or acquiring grades; grades become a *reflection* of learning rather than an acquired commodity.

From there, the tenets (and their subsequent practices) work synergistically to maximize the power of assessment within any classroom. For the purposes of this book, it is important to understand how each of the other five tenets contributes to instructional agility, as we have outlined in table I.1.

### Table I.1: Instructional Agility and the Other Assessment Tenets

| Assessment Tenet | Brief Explanation | Contribution to Instructional Agility |
|---|---|---|
| **Assessment Purpose** | Understanding assessment purpose means having a clear picture of how to use emerging assessment results. | The assessment's purpose helps clarify what assessment results teachers should use as instruction occurs. Hesitation (or a mixed message) could interfere with the necessary instructional maneuvers and student engagement as students act on feedback they receive during instruction. If the teacher is unclear about the assessment's purpose, he or she could lead students to care more about completing work than learning from their efforts and improving over time. |
| **Assessment Architecture** | Assessment is most effective when those responsible for its delivery purposefully plan it and intentionally sequence it in advance of instruction. | Planning with precision allows for maximum agility in response to emerging assessment evidence. By anticipating the most probable errors in thinking, teachers can plan their responses should those errors emerge. Identifying the most essential learning informs teachers when to make instructional moves to help students go deeper and learn more and what to revisit or let go. |
| **Accurate Interpretation** | Interpreting assessment results must be accurate, accessible, and reliable. | Instructional maneuvers are most efficient and effective when teachers accurately interpret assessment results. Clear next steps for individual students and instruction hinge on a teacher's interpretation, which he or she has generated from students' actions, dialogue, and work. Recognizing these moments is essential to accurately interpreting and providing the foundation for communicating those next steps. |

continued ➜

| Assessment Tenet | Brief Explanation | Contribution to Instructional Agility |
|---|---|---|
| **Communication of Results** | Communicating assessment results must generate productive responses from students and all stakeholders who support them. | Communicating results and next steps is essential for students to take immediate action. Opaque communication could cause an unnecessary delay in growth and achievement. Instructionally agile teachers focus on providing and facilitating next steps in learning. They must communicate this type of feedback in a way that inspires students to act and doesn't shut them down or confuse them. |
| **Student Investment** | There is a symbiotic relationship between assessment and self-regulation. | The ultimate goal is for students to be instructionally agile on their own behalf. Through self- and peer assessment they can, at best, be a more readily available source of feedback and guidance for one another. |

We explore each of these five tenets in more detail throughout the book. For now, it is important to know that it is the ways in which the tenets interconnect that maximize the power of the classroom assessment experience.

# About the Book

We know that you, who are K–12 teachers, instructional coaches, and administrators, will be at varying places in your understanding and assessment practice implementation specific to instructional agility. Some of you might have a noun-like, event-based view of assessment, while others may be further along in intentionally thinking about instructional agility. In this book, we explore the granular use of classroom assessment for instructional purposes, which means moment-to-moment, flexible assessment that occurs at the classroom level. So while we include a few points around grades and scores, as well as interim or large-scale assessments, the primary focus of *instructional agility* centers on how teachers and students use assessment results within the classroom on a daily basis.

Chapters 1 and 2 are about the culture of learning required to support instructional agility at the classroom level. Chapters 3–6 highlight the specific maneuvers teachers must employ to be agile. Finally, chapter 7 and the "Instructional Agility Manifesto" offer considerations for the beliefs and structures necessary for teachers to engage in the work of instructional agility. Each chapter begins with an instructionally agile maneuver's main ideas. These ideas include a brief synopsis of the research associated with the specific strategy. Next, we explain each maneuver *at play* or *in action* with more details. The maneuvers we offer apply to all grade levels and disciplines and may require minor adjustments for specific grade levels or content areas. The main ideas discuss the *why*, while the explanation is the *how*. From there, each chapter highlights *strategies and tools* teachers can use to be instructionally agile within that maneuver. Each chapter ends with a *conclusion* and a *pause and ponder* section, in which questions guide individual teachers and learning teams to consider potential next steps in implementation.

# Assessment Is Teaching

Teaching without assessment is not teaching; it is delivering information or creating random, haphazard activities. It is only through assessment that teachers can discern the discrepancy between a student's current understanding and the desirable performance level; it is only through assessment that teachers know what comes next for each student. The *assessment as verb* lens ensures teachers view assessment and instruction not as separate silos, but as two halves of the same whole.

Coaches are always assessing their athletes. Teaching through this lens of assessment is how teachers make real-time maneuvers to navigate instructional plans—whether that's for the next five minutes or even five days—using observations, student work, and student actions to determine if what they are doing is working. Teaching through assessment requires precision in planning, which allows maximum agility in responding to the needs of all students. We invite you to join us as we dive deeply into exploring the concepts and actions of instructional agility.

# CHAPTER 1
# ESTABLISHING A CULTURE OF LEARNING

*Research in both learning and motivation supports the
idea that classroom assessment is not solely the end point.
Rather, it is a powerful agent for influencing learning
and motivation.*

—James H. McMillan

Maintaining a classroom culture that is conducive to learning is paramount to every teacher's instructional efforts and ultimate success. Culture, a group's generally unspoken but commonly shared attitudes, beliefs, values, goals, behaviors, rituals, and social norms, can act as a lever or a roadblock to change. In other words, a teacher who intends to apply powerful strategies with instruction and assessment but does not attend to the classroom culture will most likely fail despite those strategies. If, for example, the students in a school have adopted the attitude that learning is not cool, and that culture is pervasive, then a teacher's effort to employ the best instructional strategy will have minimal impact. On the other hand, a teacher who strives to create the desired culture and then aligns instructional efforts to those shared beliefs will experience rapid change. Culture is that powerful.

When educators develop a school culture focused on learning, they have constant conversations amongst themselves and with their students about what learning looks like. They embrace mistakes and use them to better understand productive failure; they celebrate success when deep learning occurs. When a learning culture focuses on achieving mastery, teachers manage assessment processes differently by doing the following.

- Offering penalty-free practice opportunities
- Allowing mistake making and productive failure by offering feedback instead of evaluation
- Supporting growth over time by repeatedly revisiting key concepts and skills and monitoring later samples of work
- Providing culminating results that celebrate the most consistent level of achievement at the end of the learning cycle

While the proclamation that *school is about learning* sounds obvious, educators, parents, and students have not always kept a laser-like focus on the purpose of school. Traditional school culture is centered on accumulating points, climbing the (grade point average) ladder, or simply getting it done (to name just a few contradictory mindsets), all of which contribute to an opaque view of school's purpose. While most people believe that school is about learning in theory, their actions don't always match that intention. In some places, the contrast between the intent of school and how school operates sends a mixed message about what truly matters as students arrive at school each day.

Clearly, *achievement* has many definitions. While academic achievement is the most obvious outcome of the school experience, there is an implicit curriculum that influences the classroom experience, and schools benefit when they pay attention to this reality (Fisher, Frey, & Pumpian, 2012). This implicit curriculum is not the focus of this chapter (or the book), but it is, nonetheless, important to acknowledge that school is not just a clinical exercise in learning. We must also attend to socialization, personal development, and many other nonlearning attributes. Most educators know the school experience is about the whole child, which means assessment is most productive if it is planned and executed through the lens of both the cognitive and affective influences that round out every student's experience.

# The Main Idea

The growth in educators' collective understanding of the power of assessment—especially formative assessment—has brought learning back to the forefront. Teachers have transformed their practice to establish classroom environments that value students' full achievement of criteria against established standards, regardless of how low or slow they are when they begin. This shift is not yet ubiquitous; however, the pace is accelerating as more and more teachers establish new classroom routines, habits, and practices. Establishing (or returning to) a culture focused on learning is the biggest idea that sound assessment practices bring to the table, and nothing embodies that culture more than when teachers use assessment information to be instructionally agile. And although both students and teachers can influence a culture of learning, the relationship between them is significant in establishing that culture.

## Relationships Help Establish Culture

None of the assessment practices, processes, and strategies we provide in this book mean or accomplish much of anything unless teachers connect with students in meaningful, authentic ways. The adage, *students don't care how much you know until they know how much you care* has stood the test of time for a reason. Students can spot a *fake* from miles away—they know when teachers' efforts to connect are authentic or not. Taking the time and making the effort to connect are non-negotiable. While it might not be possible for teachers to get to know every student on a personal level, it is essential that teachers know students as *students*. Understanding how students learn, and relentlessly persisting and insisting they do learn, go a long way toward maximizing the impact of instruction, assessment, and feedback.

Relationships put assessment in its proper context and perspective. *Who* teachers are teaching matters more than *what* they are teaching, since teachers can't authentically get to *what* until they attend to *who*. By developing a connection to each student, teachers can begin the process of solidifying those relationships essential to maximizing learning. The truth is that assessment is relationship building. Assessment lies at the core of the learning experience for students. So, while initial efforts to establish a connection are important, the connections with students become stronger throughout the assessment process.

How teachers handle the various results of assessment speaks to the authenticity of the student-teacher relationship. The extent of the relationship is revealed during moments when students need extra time, support, or instruction. We cannot separate learning from its social context, which means assessment (and all that goes along with it) will either *contribute to* or *take away from* the established relationships between the teacher and each student.

## Culture Creates Learning

The question of which comes first—culture or learning—is worth considering. Does culture drive learning, or does the approach to learning drive culture? The short answer is *both* because teachers and students must all actively contribute. Learning is a social activity and requires social interaction, which means effective teachers respond to the intellectual and emotional needs of students in real time. Since time is always limited, being instructionally agile allows for both *efficiency* (streamlining efforts to gather sufficient and accurate information) and *effectiveness* (using the gathered information in productive and meaningful ways that promote continued learning) throughout any instructional sequence.

Though both students and teachers contribute, teachers primarily drive culture because how they design and execute instruction, and respond throughout instruction, says the most about what they value in their classrooms. Both the overt and subtle messages teachers send through their choices create the social context in which students learn. And while being cordial and friendly is desirable, how teachers handle assessment is at the core of what students experience; collegiality on the edges won't compensate for an assessment process built on completion and compliance. The integrity of classrooms (where actions match words) depends on assessment processes and practices that elevate learning to an unrivaled priority; otherwise, students won't believe their teachers when they say, "We're all about the learning."

The good news is that most teachers understand that sound assessment practices seamlessly feed a culture of learning. Clarifying learning goals, establishing transparent learning progressions, assessing *for* learning, giving effective feedback, and making corresponding instructional adjustments all make learning the clear priority. As teachers establish or reinforce these learning-centered routines, the message to students couldn't be louder or clearer—you're here to learn! Even the slightest adjustments, such as beginning each lesson by defining what students will *learn* rather than what they'll *do,* can have a significant effect in defining activities and tasks by the ends rather than the means.

Being or becoming instructionally agile is essential to establishing a new kind of learning culture. Nothing sends a stronger message than when the teacher is prepared to respond—often in real time—to assessment results that reveal where the student *is* compared to where he or she is *going.* Teachers can match their words to their actions by giving classroom assessments that result in student-responsive instructional adjustments. By planning for these potential adjustments, teachers establish a *new normal* in which their verbal and nonverbal responses communicate that learning is fluid, ongoing, and even non-negotiable.

## Learning Creates Culture

At the same time, students themselves can and do contribute greatly to the culture of any classroom, so they solidify the classroom culture through their learning. Students aren't widgets, so seeking a singularly prescribed culture of learning is nearly impossible, even though some principles and practices are associated with the most favorable courses of action. Teachers can set up opportunities to learn, but it's up to the students to follow through, since culture emerges from the sum of their collective experiences. When students do not follow through, an instructionally agile teacher makes another move to influence them. Teachers must set up these opportunities to learn and continually try new instructional maneuvers to impact learning and confidence.

Every learning theory includes some form of regulation by the student (Brookhart, 2013a). The true test of a positive classroom culture is students' ability to become instructionally agile and regulate their own learning. When students believe they can control the outcome of the learning process, they are more likely to learn. This might seem obvious, but students can—and do—often attribute their success to that which is external, unstable, and uncontrollable (Weiner, 1979).

For example, students who believe an assessment was easy are attributing their success to something beyond their control both in the moment and going forward. They think they are only successful if and when the teacher randomly adjusts the assessment experience. When students realize that they owe their success to internal, stable, and controlled factors (that they had everything to do with succeeding), teachers create an environment in which students expect to succeed. When they expect to succeed—when they expect to learn—a culture of learning begins to override other perspectives (for example, they got lucky or the teacher is easy) that too often dominate the classroom experience.

A culture of learning focuses on the process of learning, not just the final summative assessment score. A culture of learning, therefore, is also a culture of *thinking*. Teachers have the power to implement various forces to shape that kind of culture.

## Forces That Shape a Culture of Thinking

In *Creating Cultures of Thinking: The 8 Forces We Must Master to Truly Transform Our Schools*, Ron Ritchhart (2015) outlines the eight cultural forces that impact how teachers create environments of thinking. According to Ritchhart (2015), each of these forces can, if teachers intentionally implement them, shape a classroom culture that encourages thinking and deeper levels of engagement. Eliciting evidence of thinking is assessment at its best. A *culture of thinking* is an environment in which assessment maximizes the process of learning by allowing teachers to be agile in developing the opportunities for students to think more deeply.

Table 1.1 outlines Ritchhart's eight cultural forces that imbue every classroom with a culture of thinking (Ritchhart, 2015).

*Table 1.1: Eight Cultural Forces*

| Force | Brief Explanation |
|---|---|
| Time | Allocate time for thinking by providing chances to explore topics in more depth as well as to formulate thoughtful responses. |
| Opportunities | Provide purposeful activities that require students to engage in thinking and developing understanding as part of their ongoing classroom experience. |

continued ➜

| Force | Brief Explanation |
|---|---|
| **Routines and Structures** | Scaffold students' thinking in the moment as well as provide tools and teach patterns of thinking students can use independently. |
| **Language** | Use a language of thinking that provides students with the vocabulary for describing and reflecting on thinking. |
| **Modeling** | Model who you are as thinkers and students so you discuss, share, and make visible the process of thinking. |
| **Interactions and Relationships** | Show respect for and value one another's contributions of ideas and thinking in a spirit of ongoing collaborative inquiry. |
| **Physical Environment** | Make thinking visible by displaying the process of thinking and development of ideas. Arrange the space to facilitate thoughtful interactions. |
| **Expectations** | Set an agenda of understanding and convey clear expectations. Focus on the value of thinking and learning as outcomes as opposed to mere completion of work. |

Each of these forces has very real assessment implications that can impact how instructionally agile teachers can be as they respond to the emerging evidence of students' thinking. Creating a culture of learning by examining assessment through the lens of these eight forces fosters an environment in which students can potentially come to see themselves as partners in the learning process. Table 1.2 outlines the same eight cultural forces in the classroom with their implications for assessment.

### Table 1.2: Assessment Implications of the Eight Cultural Forces

| Force | Assessment Implications |
|---|---|
| **Time** | Assessment is more about *quality* than quantity, so while speed and ease are always desirable, effectiveness must be the primary goal. Students need ample time to think, process, and rethink throughout instruction. |
| **Opportunities** | Teachers must have student *thinking* in mind when designing quality assessments that consistently provide opportunities for students to display—and even track—their thinking. This means assessment design moves beyond just a single test to more organic, engaging, and authentic performance tasks. |
| **Routines and Structures** | Assessment routines and structures anchored on clear learning intentions, success criteria, and learning progressions create predictable instructional decisions that allow for scaffolding toward proficiency. |

| Language | The language of assessment can lead students toward a deeper level of thinking. Assessing *why* (and the interconnectedness of standards) instead of simply *what* allows for an integrated assessment approach. |
|---|---|
| Modeling | Through instruction and assessment, teachers can make their thinking visible by modeling the potential approaches students can take to grow in their learning and the struggle that often comes with thinking deeply. Modeling this struggle helps students better understand the experience they may have as they think deeply. |
| Interactions and Relationships | Assessment is relationship building. How teachers create assessments and respond to their results reveals the true nature of the student-teacher relationship. Teachers do not accept students' failure to do the work and persistently provide feedback and scaffolded support to promote student achievement. |
| Physical Environment | Using exemplars gives students potential opportunities to demonstrate their thinking. Teachers guide them to examine the qualities of thinking within the exemplars and advise them to avoid mimicking what they're seeing, hearing, or touching. |
| Expectations | Setting learning intentions, success criteria, and the progression to proficiency solidifies expectations for success. When teachers put in place these clear expectations for performance at a greater depth of knowledge, they make it clear to students that memorization and recall fall short of the ultimate goal. |

These forces are integral to every teachers' efforts to be precise yet flexible in all assessment efforts. The eight cultural forces must be considered as teachers implement any instructionally agile maneuver described in the following chapters. Any maneuver may work or not work to create a culture of learning, and it is often these forces that may prevent the maneuver from working well. Chapter 2 discusses how to engineer dialogue and engage in conversations to gather and respond to evidence of learning. Chapter 3 focuses on eliciting evidence through questioning. Observation is key to instructional agility, so chapter 4 explores this means of gathering evidence. Chapter 5 discusses mobilizing students to be instructionally agile on their own. Practicing is central to instructional agility, so chapter 6 illustrates various ways that practice provides opportunities for teachers to be instructionally agile. This includes shaping the role homework plays in instructional agility. Educators often debate the value of homework in supporting learning, so it's necessary to tackle this important dilemma. Finally, chapter 7 discusses the broader context and how jurisdictions, districts, schools, and teams can be instructionally agile. The elements of these forces are front and center as teachers maximize the opportunity to be agile in response to every student, developing a rich culture of learning.

# A Culture of Learning in Action

Instructional agility doesn't just happen. Teachers must intentionally strive to be agile in response to the evidence of learning that they uncover during the assessment process. Planning for flexibility creates an assessment dichotomy with which teachers must become comfortable; the notion of planning for flexible responses seems odd and yet, it is the essence of instructional agility.

While it may seem like a paradox, instructional agility is anchored in the process of *planning with precision*, which leads to a *response with maximum flexibility*. Certainly, teachers cannot know how each student is going to respond to assessment opportunities, but they can anticipate the most typical understandings and misunderstandings students will demonstrate. Most teachers have a clear picture of the most likely results. The greater the precision in planning, the greater the opportunity in responding to meet each student's needs. It is a front-back relationship—if teachers invest in front-end planning there is a back-end payoff of more effective and intentional instructional responses with higher achievement.

To create an instructionally agile learning environment, teachers can do a lot with design, interpretation, and response. While the remaining chapters in this book examine specific strategies teachers can use to intentionally elicit evidence and allow for maximum response agility, we explore the prerequisites in design, interpretation, and response in the following sections. We do not intend to explore each of the strategies in depth; rather, we explore strategies and prerequisites within the context of creating a culture of learning. It is one thing to have a friendly, engaging environment, but it's quite another to go a step further to create a real culture that puts *learning* at the center of the student experience. From an assessment perspective, the following strategies and constructs make the words *learning-centered culture* a reality in the classroom: assessment design, accurate interpretation, and assessment response.

## Assessment Design

Developing a culture of learning is an intentional process that begins with planning assessment outcomes. A true culture of learning makes learning the centerpiece of what students experience every day. This is the basis of the assessment architecture tenet. The following four criteria are crucial to developing a culture of learning.

1. Clear learning intentions

2. Clear success criteria

3. Learning progressions

4. Quality, learning-centered tasks

## Clear Learning Intentions

A culture of learning begins by clarifying what students are supposed to *learn* through instruction. This is different than simply advising students on what they are going to *do*, since the activities they participate in are more the means than the end. Whether teachers post, communicate orally, or demonstrate learning intentions, it is vital that students are clear on the intended learning so they understand why the teacher is asking them to do particular activities or tasks.

Students often ask their teachers *why* they have to do, know, or show things, which can be a sign that the learning intentions are not explicit. The question is not whether teachers teach with clear learning intentions in mind; they do. But they often do not clearly articulate those learning intentions to students. Once students are clear on the intended results of the learning experience—skills, concepts, or even dispositions— they will see that there is a *learning purpose* behind the activities and assignments.

## Clear Success Criteria

Success criteria describe the qualities of what exemplary work, performances, or tangible demonstrations look like. Here is where teachers describe—in sufficient detail—what students will *do* to meet the intended learning outcomes; the two go hand in hand. Learning intentions describe *what* they will learn, while success criteria describe *how they will show* what they've learned. Teachers can communicate success criteria orally or through examples, demonstrations, simulations, rubrics, and checklists. The advantages to each method depend on the learning goals. Performance assessments lend themselves nicely to rubrics and demonstrations, while a written composition might use a rubric along with a handful of exemplars.

The critical aspect of establishing and communicating success criteria is that they be substantive rather than trivial (Brookhart, 2007). Establishing success criteria with students must be part of a larger process with the goal of student engagement throughout the assessment experience (Andrade, 2013). Co-constructing success criteria, goal setting for individual demonstrations of learning, self-assessment, and peer assessment are all examples of how to engage students directly through assessment. (We will explore this concept in depth in chapter 5, page 99.) To establish a culture of learning, teachers must provide a clear description of what that learning will look like by articulating clear, specific success criteria. Nothing screams learning like directly communicating *this is what your learning will look like.*

## Learning Progressions

A *learning progression* is an intentional sequence of learning goals and success criteria that teachers form into a model to lead students from the simplest to the most sophisticated understandings. The truth is that most teachers teach with some kind of learning progression in mind, but it's less common to articulate that progression to the students. It is equally rare for a teacher to use the students' assessment evidence, which illustrates where each student is in understanding the planned instructional responses. Transparency at all stages leads to understanding and engagement. Also known as *learning trajectories* or *construct maps*, progressions of learning provide the necessary model of cognition that so many assessment systems and processes seem to lack by outlining typical development over time (Brown & Wilson, 2011). Whether teachers develop the progressions through a top-down or bottom-up process (Heritage, 2013), they are essential for showing students that there is a path to reach advanced or exemplary levels of understanding.

Teachers develop *top-down progressions* (starting with the end in mind and then backward-mapping the steps it would take for a learner to get to the standard) from what they know about learning within any discipline and from their background and a research base, which does not always exist in every subject. Teachers develop *bottom-up progressions* (observing learning as it happens and noting what comes first, second, third, and so on) more organically based on their collective experience in how students typically progress toward the most sophisticated level of understanding.

According to Margaret Heritage (2013), a "by-product of teacher-developed progressions is an associated deepening of teacher knowledge about learning in a domain, which can have considerable payoff for evidence gathering and use" (p. 189). This assessment payoff is why teachers should be hands-on when it comes to assessment design. The truth is that teachers likely use a hybrid approach to develop learning progressions, which considers what available research says about learning within a discipline and pairing it with teacher experience to formulate the most efficient and effective approach to instruction and assessment.

## Quality, Learning-Centered Tasks

Establishing a culture of learning means teachers must elicit evidence through quality, learning-centered tasks. When teachers ask students to engage in activities that directly relate to the learning intentions, success criteria, and learning progressions, students feel respected and see the school experience as purposeful and coherent. Respectful tasks and activities meet students where they are, meaning that no matter their level readiness, they have a clear path to achieving the grade-level standard and beyond. Teachers have—or can at least envision—what it means to assign students busywork that is only loosely connected to the intended learning and progression. Activities should focus on essential understandings and create opportunities for each student to engage in his or her learning at a high level.

## Accurate Interpretation

Teachers can establish a culture of learning through the interpretation phase of assessment as well. Interpreting assessment results—and the subsequent action—can spur the potential maneuvers necessary for students' continued improvement. To keep learning at the center, teachers use strategies, practices, and processes that trigger a learning-focused response from students. The following components are essential in creating a culture of learning through accurate assessment interpretation: feedback, time to act, and expectations for feedback.

### Feedback

The epicenter of a culture focused on learning is the practice of providing students with feedback that describes how their learning can continue. That said, feedback does not always create a culture of learning because not all feedback puts continual growth at the heart of its purpose. Grades, as an example, are technically a kind of feedback, but a letter grade does not include information about what comes next in the learning progression. Despite their current necessity for reporting achievement, grades (in whatever form or format they might be) are generally not effective feedback to improve learning. Also, *confirmation* or *compliance* feedback (in other words, did the student complete the task?) is typically void of any meaningful description of quality and how students might improve that quality. Providing these types of feedback is simply not enough.

Teachers who use assessment to create a culture of learning purposefully describe what students need to do to continue their learning trajectory. The research on feedback is relatively clear that symbols, such as grades, scores, or levels, have the potential to interfere with student willingness to keep learning (Butler, 1988; Wiliam, 2011). High-performing learners often check their grades; if these do not meet their expectations, sometimes they want to do more activities or find alternate ways to acquire more points to get a better grade. They miss the idea that improving quality or revising current work using the teacher's comments is what will improve the grade. Some high-performing learners just settle for what they have, ignoring the feedback because the initial score indicates a level of satisfactory achievement. Struggling learners often give up and likewise ignore feedback because the initial score indicates a level of unsatisfactory achievement. This means the most favorable course of action, especially when building a culture of learning, is to provide feedback in lieu of a grade, score, or level; this allows both the teacher and student the optimal conditions under which to be instructionally agile while moving toward proficiency.

### Time to Act

A culture focused on learning allows time to act on feedback. Providing effective feedback is essential. However, if students don't get time to act on the feedback, the feedback is effectively useless and the message they receive is that growth is not a priority. This is easier said than done given the volume and nature of the standards and curriculum. This is something to understand but should not act as an excuse. The standards or the curriculum cannot interfere with learning, which means teachers must allot time, regardless of how scarce it may be, for students to absorb, reflect, and act on the feedback they receive. Intentionally prioritizing the learning goals that are the focus of this targeted feedback is the solution to this persistent dilemma.

### Expectations for Feedback

In a culture of learning, students expect feedback and know its sole purpose is to guide their continual growth. Students don't see feedback as criticism; rather, they recognize it as an opportunity to move to the next level. As well, teachers who actively work to create a culture of learning consistently expect that students *use* the feedback they receive. Teachers often complain that students don't use their feedback. When we ask students if there is a specific routine that instructs them how to act on feedback, their answer is often *no*. Creating a habit of learning is about creating an expectation of learning, and the most effective learning-centered cultures don't allow students to opt out.

## Assessment Response

Conducting assessments is good, but responding to assessment results is even better. How teachers respond to assessment results goes a long way toward establishing and maintaining a culture of learning in which students, again, see assessment as an opportunity rather than an event. The response should include both differentiation and grading.

### Differentiation

Like feedback, differentiation is a mainstay in a culture of learning because it makes both the student and the learning priorities. Being a student-responsive teacher sends a clear signal that learning—not coverage—matters most. Differentiation is, in essence, an instructionally agile model that teachers maximize when their response to assessment evidence meets the needs of each student, whether that need is extension, further instruction, or acute intervention. According to Carol Ann Tomlinson and Tonya R. Moon (2013), differentiating assessment means that "the learning outcomes remain the same . . . while the format of assessment, time allowance, and scaffolding may vary" (p. 417). A culture of learning grows when teachers use assessment to seek understanding of student background, readiness, interest, and approach to learning.

Readiness gives teachers the potential to be instructionally agile. Knowing what new learning a student is ready for maximizes the efficiency and effectiveness of postassessment maneuvers. Whether through preassessment or ongoing formative assessment, teachers can be more agile in responding to student needs and can accelerate the establishment of a culture of learning. Throughout the remaining chapters, we offer strategies, practices, and processes teachers can use to elicit evidence of student readiness, making instructional agility more possible.

## Grading

How teachers grade—how they verify that learning has occurred and report that information to others—will either contribute to or take away from a culture of learning. Common sense dictates that a culture of learning produces grades that reflect that learning—nothing more and nothing less. It may seem obvious that a culture of learning and grades that encompass nonlearning or behavioral factors do not align, but there is still considerable debate about the modernization of grading practices, since the research on standards-based grading is in its infancy (Brookhart, 2013b).

There is not enough space in this book to thoroughly explore the move to learning-centered grades (or grades based on achieving standards), but should you have questions, you can refer to the countless professional resources available for details on how to create a learning-centered grading system (Guskey, 2015; O'Connor, 2011; Reeves, 2016; Schimmer, 2016; Schimmer, Hillman, & Stalets, in press). Visit **go.SolutionTree .com/assessment** for links to these resources. Despite the pockets of debate, we strongly believe a culture of learning is a culture in which student grades exclusively reflect their levels of achievement.

# Strategies and Tools

The focus of this book is about making instructional maneuvers yet teachers cannot maximize those maneuvers without firmly establishing a culture of learning. This section offers a few practical ways in which teachers can begin or maintain a culture that values *who* they teach more than *what* they teach.

## Strategy 1: Design Assessments

Designing assessments is not just a procedural exercise; there is a human side to assessment that teachers must always be mindful of. Assessments will either add to or take away from the student-teacher relationship. Assessments that are sensitive to student readiness are the ones that help build strong, trusting relationships.

As well, paralanguage—elements that accompany spoken words—is critical, since not all learning demonstrations emerge in written form, which means *how* students communicate their learning provides additional insight. Listening to the *tone* of a response or watching student body language while solving a difficult problem can be influential on how teachers respond in real time. And finally, knowing *why* an assessment is occurring and how the teacher intends to use the results gives the necessary transparency that allows students to invest in the assessment experience.

## Build Strong Relationships

It may seem odd that building relationships falls under assessment design, but as we have already established, we cannot separate learning from its social context, which means the relationships teachers have with students undoubtedly impact the culture of learning. Teachers can begin by making a personal connection with their students. This doesn't mean teachers become best friends with every student, but it does mean getting to know each student on a somewhat personal level. They can ask students questions about themselves, their families, hobbies, the way they learn, and the way they do not learn.

Teachers can also reveal a personal side of themselves that humanizes the classroom experience. They may model moments of frustration, perseverance, and success, showing students their own intimate understanding of the learning process. In a culture of learning that maximizes the opportunity for teachers to be instructionally agile (and for students to engage in carrying out the subsequent actions), teachers and students invest in one another and trust that the relationship is strong enough to withstand—even prevent—any potentially aversive situations or circumstances.

## Be Mindful of Paralanguage

Certainly, what teachers say goes a long way toward communicating priorities, but of equal influence on a culture of learning is their *paralanguage*—all the things that accompany words, like body language, pitch, and tone. Whether it's tone of voice, certain gestures, facial expressions, or other nonverbal forms of communication, teachers who are mindful of aligning language and paralanguage help solidify a culture of learning. The messages to students about the importance of learning ring hollow if nonverbal cues say the opposite. For example, a teacher who offers further opportunities to deepen understanding, but does so with a tone of frustration, may send a mixed message: Is it okay to take longer to learn or isn't it? Students who struggle or simply take longer to complete their work can be quite sensitive to paralanguage, so just being aware of the alignment between verbal and nonverbal messages increases the likelihood of creating an optimal learning environment.

## Stay Focused on the Why

So much of the frustration students experience in school centers on the lack of clarity they have about why they are doing what they do. Too often, we expect students to complete tasks, assignments, and other activities without understanding *why* they're doing them and what it will eventually lead to. Teachers who build cultures of learning do so by making the learning intentions and success criteria transparent, as well as continually explaining how *today* meshes with the overarching goals of *tomorrow* (the learning progression).

By articulating clear learning intentions, specific targets, and success criteria, teachers keep learning at the forefront. They can also frame any other skill-based or attribute-based learning in terms of *why* when they, for example, organize students into groups to produce tangible evidence of learning (such as a project) as well as learn how to function within an effective collaborative team. In this case, teachers don't leave students wondering why they are doing group work to produce evidence of learning; they know that the process of learning effective collaboration is a parallel learning goal.

# Strategy 2: Interpret Assessments

Assessment's power comes from *using* the results to advance student learning, but for results to be used productively, teachers must communicate results with a learning-centered focus (and the necessary finesse) to ensure students keep learning. After interpreting assessments, teachers can engineer opportunities for students to actively advance their own proficiency. Providing feedback that focuses on what's next causes thinking and balances both strengths and that which needs strengthening. Teachers can feel more confident that students will see assessment interpretation as simply the next opportunity to expand their skills and understandings.

## Emphasize What's Next

Instructional agility is all about *what's next*, so assessing through that lens is essential. Feedback and subsequent actions are more effective when they describe rather than evaluate, especially when teachers intend to use assessments formatively. For example, teachers can begin feedback with the phrase, "Now let's work on . . ." instead of "You should have . . ." Though it may seem subtle, this level of awareness not only addresses the *what's next* view of feedback, but its paralanguage also aligns. For example, consider the following: "Now let's work on isolating the variable before dividing both sides by four." This sounds more learning centered than, "You should have isolated the variable before dividing both sides by four." One is descriptive, and the other is judgmental.

## Promote Thinking Opportunities

As we discussed earlier, one of the cultural forces that shape classrooms is the *opportunity* students have to think (Ritchhart, 2015). Teachers provide consistent opportunities for students to think by stimulating them with feedback. Feedback that takes the form of a cue, question, or prompt directs student attention to the appropriate place but asks students to determine why. For example, a teacher may ask a student why he or she has highlighted a particular passage in a writing sample. Asking questions instead of providing answers *forces* students to be active participants in the feedback process because they find the details of the feedback in the answers. Even more, actively involving students in the process of self- and peer assessment requires them to think throughout the entire assessment process. Learning is thinking, so by using strategies that force students to think, teachers instill in them the primary concern that *more learning* should emerge from any initial demonstration.

## Balance Strengths and Areas Needing Improvement

Taking a balanced approach to feedback sends the message that *everyone is somewhere on the path to proficiency.* For students who are more confident and more proficient, a deficiency focus may not be problematic, but for others, the deficiency focus may inadvertently embed an *I can't* mindset. It's not hard to imagine how much it affects a student's psyche to only hear what's wrong. This would negatively impact the confidence and motivation of many adults, let alone students. By balancing both strengths and areas needing improvement (and by ensuring that *all* students experience a similar process), teachers send the message that everyone is a student and that addressing areas needing improvement is what students do.

# Strategy 3: Respond to Assessments

Assessment result use doesn't just happen. After interpreting and communicating, teachers can create or embed routines of correction within their classrooms. By creating an expectation of correction, teachers will proactively send the message that learning is continual, regardless of what an assessment reveals, and that correcting errors is a natural part of learning. Even still, creating collaborative correction habits undercuts any competitive aspects of assessment by overtly supporting the notion that everyone can and will contribute to all learning.

## Create the Routine of Correction

Teachers who create routines and habits of responding to feedback and correcting errors can instill a learning mindset in their students. When teachers build instructional correctives into typical routines, they make it clear that they anticipate some error and there will be more to do postassessment. Using feedback is where the real power of formative assessment lies, and when students come to know *how* to go about making improvements, they can maximize opportunities going forward. Planning to be instructionally agile includes creating routines of correction after eliciting evidence. Through self-assessment, students can also discover what needs improvement. (We explore self-assessment in more depth in chapter 5, page 99.) For now, know that establishing a culture of learning includes planning for *more* learning through corrective action on the students' part.

## Use Collaborative Corrections

Students don't have to go at it alone; corrections and responses can be a collective effort. The benefit for all students is exposure to the wide range of perspectives available within any given classroom. This can be part of the peer assessment process, or it can be a stand-alone process of collective response to teacher-based assessment. Again, the message of anticipated error can put all students at ease since the teacher will require a postassessment response from them. In addition, the collaborative correction process can create an *everyone helps everyone* culture that can counter the inherent competitive environment in some classrooms. Collaboration can occur in a reciprocal partnership or within an entire group in which all students collectively respond to assessment evidence. Either way, having access to others' thoughts on how to improve only adds to a culture squarely focused on learning for all.

# Conclusion

Being instructionally agile is contingent on a culture of learning. Learning creates culture, and culture influences learning, so intentionality is key to evolving a classroom culture away from a *task completion* mindset. Completing tasks is important, of course, but implicit in the *task completion* mindset is the idea that completing the task is the end, not the means. Real-time instructional maneuvers lean heavily on a norm of correction and growth. When students believe learning is eventually possible, they are more likely to invest at all points (design, interpretation, and response) along the way.

Both teachers and students nurture and develop cultures of learning, and while it might seem obvious that a culture of learning focuses on *learning*, without the habitual processes connected to learning goals, success criteria, learning progressions, feedback, correctives, and expected growth, a culture of learning is unlikely to emerge. A culture truly anchored in learning means viewing evidence of learning (and the corresponding instructional maneuvers) as an opportunity rather than an onerous event.

# Pause and Ponder

Take a few moments to reflect on the following questions.

- In your classroom or school, does learning create culture or does culture influence learning? Explain.

- Of the eight forces that transform classrooms (see table 1.1, page 15), which ones represent areas of strength in your classroom or school? Which ones do you think need more attention in your classroom or school?

- When was the last time you used assessment evidence to make real-time instructional maneuvers? Describe what you did, why you did it, and the impact it had on students.

- How consistently do you communicate learning intentions, success criteria, and learning progressions? Is there more you could do to embed these aspects into your assessment routines?

- Is the *time to act* on feedback proportional to the *amount of feedback* you provide to students?

# CHAPTER 2
# ENGINEERING ENGAGING CONVERSATIONS

*The feeling of being interested can act as a kind of*
*neurological signal, directing us to fruitful areas of inquiry.*

—B. F. Skinner

The practice of engineering engaging conversations in the classroom provides a significant foundation for a successful culture of learning. Despite its invaluable contribution to learning, the process of engineering engaging conversations is completely underused when it comes to making real-time instructional adjustments. Teachers should not consider dialogue or active, social learning as strategies for rare occasions. Rather, engaging conversations should happen intentionally and consistently, not merely when it is convenient or when students seem ready. In other words, working collaboratively with peers in a learning context is vital to the process of learning and is imperative to being instructionally agile. Engineering engaging conversations marks a change in modern teaching and learning, as even direct instruction must include a pathway of provocative questions and compelling conversations that students drive themselves.

# The Main Idea

Dylan Wiliam (2011) notes that engineering engaging conversations is a critical formative assessment practice. What does it mean to engineer conversations? During instruction, teachers design engaging conversations (for example, topics of interest, worthy questions, collective inquiry, provoked thinking, collaborative learning) within a wide variety of discussion formats, such as Socratic seminars, philosophical chairs, debates, and juried forums, and varied groupings (large group, small group, and one-on-one options), as a primary means of helping students explore the concepts at hand. While direct instruction provides the easiest pathway for dispersing key concepts and is the most teacher-controlled option for dispensing and then monitoring learning, it can fall short of helping students make meaning as they do when teachers invite them to co-create understanding with their peers through conversations. There are five significant reasons why a culture of learning must embrace engaging conversations as a cultural expectation and a core instructional practice. The first three benefit students, while the last two benefit teachers.

1. Developing speaking and listening skills
2. Promoting productive group work
3. Co-creating meaning
4. Gathering emerging evidence
5. Shifting power

Teachers benefit when students do the heavy lifting during the instructional process. When students control the conversation, it frees teachers from the demands of thinking ahead to the next instructional decision while they are in the midst of delivering direct instruction. It also provides more time for teachers to observe and interpret emerging evidence, making them more apt to respond with precision and flexibility along the way.

## Develop Speaking and Listening Skills

Communication is a critical skill. It involves sharing thoughts, feelings, ideas, questions, concerns, and solutions in healthy and productive ways. While writing is an important medium for communicating, speaking and listening are far more common in the average person's daily life. Virtually every state, province, region, and country has education standards for speaking and listening. Modern standards require students to be able to accomplish the following communication skills.

- Communicate coherent instructions.

- Express thoughts clearly.

- Crisply articulate opinions.

- Analyze and frame effective arguments.

- Maintain a sustained conversation over a period of time with diverse audiences.

- Motivate others through powerful speech.

Speaking and listening are critical 21st century communication skills and, as such, are relevant for study in every discipline, subject, and grade level. Revised standards, written to target the next generation's needs at the state, provincial, and national levels, consistently require high levels of discourse in all subjects as the bridge between inputs (such as reading, viewing, listening, or observing) and outputs (such as writing, speaking, creating, or solving). When it comes to speaking and listening, there is much to learn. As the world continues to shrink through global interdependence and connectedness, the skills of clear communication and civil discourse continue to grow in importance.

## *Promote Productive Group Work*

Engineering conversations involves employing constructs for collaborative group work in which teams work together to reach a common goal, capitalize on each team member's strengths, and achieve a greater purpose. Like speaking and listening, productive group work is a 21st century skill or crosscurricular competency. The National Education Association (n.d.) states:

> Generally, collaboration has been accepted as a skill that's essential to achieve meaningful and effective results. In the past decade, however, it has become increasingly clear that collaboration is not only important but necessary for students and employees, due to globalization and the rise of technology. (p. 19)

To engineer conversations, teachers must do more than simply design interesting questions worth discussing; it involves employing robust, provocative, and meaningful questions that elicit *observable* evidence. This allows teachers to have access to student thinking that in turn allows them to respond with agility.

The Common Core State Standards (National Governors Association Center for Best Practices [NGA] & Council of Chief State School Officers [CCSSO], 2010) highlight some of the following features of productive group work:

- Participate in collaborative conversations with diverse partners . . . (SL.2.1)
- Follow agreed-upon rules for discussions . . . (SL.2.1a)
- Initiate and participate effectively in a range of collaborative discussions . . . (SL.9–10.1)
- Come to discussions prepared, having read and researched material under study; explicitly draw on that preparation by referring to evidence from texts and other research on the topic or issue to stimulate a thoughtful, well-reasoned exchange of ideas. (SL.9–10.1a)
- Work with peers to set rules for collegial discussions and decision making (e.g., informal consensus, taking votes on key issues, presentation of alternate views), clear goals and deadlines, and individual roles as needed. (SL.9–10.1b)
- Respond thoughtfully to diverse perspectives, summarize points of agreement and disagreement, and, when warranted, qualify or justify views and understanding and make new connections in light of the evidence and reasoning presented. (SL.9–10.1d)

Students of all ages must be able to speak in one-to-one situations, in small groups, in large groups, with people older than themselves, with peers, with individuals with whom they share ideology, and with individuals with whom they disagree. Moreover, they must understand the rules of quality discussions and follow protocols for different dialogue constructs.

According to Robert J. Marzano (2007), collaborative or cooperative learning is one of the most powerful instructional options a teacher has in the classroom. Most industries today value the idea of working—and learning—collaboratively. Education is no exception, as teachers engage in the work of professional learning communities (PLCs; DuFour, DuFour, & Eaker, 2008; DuFour, DuFour, Eaker, Many, & Mattos, 2016). Don Tapscott (2013), chancellor of Trent University, notes the following during his commencement speech to the graduating classes of business and nursing:

> Collaboration is important not just because it's a better way to learn. The spirit of collaboration is penetrating every institution and all of our lives. So learning to collaborate is part of equipping yourself for effectiveness, problem solving, innovation and life-long learning in an ever-changing networked economy.

Students' success is based on their ability to survive in a workforce that demands productive group work. That means teachers must engineer thought-provoking conversations with an assessment mindset in order to provide students with real-time next steps.

## Co-Create Meaning

Making meaning does not happen in a vacuum. No matter their age, students generally need to grapple with their understandings to create meaning and better refine their grasp of concepts. Many instructional theories (for example, project-based learning, constructivism, inquiry-based education, and authentic intellectual instruction) have attempted to capture this notion for classroom teachers:

> After the late 1980s, theory and research increasingly emphasized inquiry-based instructional models, in which the teacher's most important role was in designing lessons or learning experiences that involved guiding students toward new understanding through exploration and induction. (Louis, Leithwood, Wahlstrom, & Anderson, 2010, pp. 38–39)

Conversation, through exploration and inquiry, is essential for students to co-create meaning of their learning.

Peer-to-peer modeling can occur as students co-create meaning. Douglas Fisher and Nancy Frey (2010) and John Hattie (2009) note that ability grouping can be detrimental to students' self-esteem and efficacy, so intentionally creating diverse groups is important to ensure each team's success and each student's opportunity to continue to learn: "As part of their interaction, productive group members share information and experiences, thus building each other's background knowledge" (Fisher & Frey, 2010, p. 118). When teachers place students in mixed-ability groups to grapple with difficult concepts, struggling students, nonreaders, and second language students immerse themselves in a steady dose of:

- Access to academic language (a deficit in vocabulary knowledge is a major obstacle to academic achievement)

- Opportunities to hear and observe how students think and explore complex material

- Exposure to complex material that they may not have otherwise accessed through personal reading

Likewise, in mixed groupings, strong readers and skilled students gain access to:

- Clarity about potential pitfalls, misunderstandings, and misconceptions

- Deeper understanding through instructive conversations and alternate perspectives

- Increased empathy for others managing intellectual challenges

Co-creating meaning benefits all students. And it works in all subjects.

*All* students experience the benefits of quality discussions. Mathematics experts Suzanne Chapin, Cathy O'Conner, and Nancy Anderson (2013) suggest there are five major benefits to using talk in the mathematics classroom:

1. Talk can reveal understanding and misunderstanding.
2. Talk supports robust learning by boosting memory.
3. Talk supports deeper reasoning.
4. Talk supports language development.
5. Talk supports development of social skills. (p. xv)

The list of benefits is so compelling that it's fair to say that talk is critical to teaching and learning in any subject.

Quiet classrooms are not always the most conducive places for students to learn, nor do they support teachers being instructionally agile because student thinking is hidden from them. Meaningful discussions have a potential benefit to both students and teachers. A better option involves organized chaos, in which teams of students grapple with difficult concepts and collaborate to explore and solve complex problems.

Of course, not all opportunities to talk are valuable. Therefore, it's critical that teachers engineer these conversations, teach the process of conducting quality learning conversations, and then engage students in monitoring and adjusting for their own effectiveness in those desired conversations. It requires constant mental and dual processing. Students create meaning when they actively reflect on the following five elements during any learning conversation.

1. Their thoughts and feelings about the topic at hand
2. The evidence and arguments they can use to support their perspective
3. Their personal effectiveness in productive group work
4. Their personal communication strengths and stretches
5. Their mental shifts in understanding over time and the causes of those shifts

Engaging conversations are beneficial to all students—especially *teachers* as students. When teachers can listen to the thinking around them, they are generally more open to feedback and more reflective on their own effectiveness as the learning occurs.

## Gather Emerging Evidence

Instructionally agile teachers are aware of and respond to emerging evidence. They seek evidence of learning in both nonverbal and verbal forms so they can isolate and clarify simple mistakes, errors in reasoning, or misconceptions while capitalizing on moments of clarity and accuracy. Engineering engaging conversations is as much about putting students into formal discussion constructs (such as forums, seminars, and debates) around specific topics as it is about activating students as resources for one another as they diagnose learning through co-constructing criteria for quality, collaboratively scoring, peer reviewing, and providing feedback (Chappuis, 2014; Wiliam, 2011). When teachers listen to students talking about learning, they can make informed decisions about each student's degree of proficiency.

More important, by listening as the learning unfolds, teachers can turn simple mistakes, errors, or misconceptions into true learning opportunities by engaging the entire classroom in diagnosing and problem solving common patterns in those areas—that's instructional agility. Students are less likely to repeat common errors when they are clear about what to anticipate and avoid.

Such work requires a high degree of finesse on the part of the teachers. At no point should they ever expose, embarrass, or shame any student for mistakes they make along the learning path. They must build the work of engineering conversations on the firm foundation of collaboration and trust so that the classroom environment is risk free and everyone views mistakes as normal opportunities to improve. Emerging evidence can provide just-in-time fodder for individual and classroom feedback as learning occurs.

## Shift Power

Schools should not be places where students go to watch teachers work exceptionally hard. The tables need to turn so that students are doing more of the mental heavy lifting. In order for that to happen, teachers must thoughtfully engage students in meaningful learning opportunities that require them to experience disciplined inquiry. Moreover, with increasing ease of access to expanding information and worldviews, teachers can no longer be the sole keepers of knowledge and learning. Instead, teachers must facilitate learning conversations in which students gather, interpret, discuss, explore, debate, challenge, and refine each other's ideas.

Students must research thoroughly, cite sources consistently, reason logically, argue persuasively, and, ultimately, inspire change. They should practice this work through collaborative learning experiences with consistency from classroom to classroom, grade level to grade level, and discipline to discipline. When teachers shift the power to students for collective inquiry and the co-construction of meaning, they can activate modern standards while simultaneously increasing student investment.

When teachers use engaging conversations as a mainstay for instruction, everyone in the classroom can engage in instructional agility. Options for observing, questioning, probing, modeling, practicing, and mobilizing learning increase, and teachers gain the space to diagnose and respond to the emerging evidence.

## Connections to Other Tenets

The work of creating a learning-rich culture through engineering engaging conversations is foundational. As such, it easily taps into all six assessment tenets (Erkens et al., 2017). Three of those are integral to the work of engineering conversations: assessment purpose, instructional agility, and student investment.

When it comes to engineering engaging conversations, the assessment purposes are truly interdependent. Classroom conversations can and should be both formative and summative. Teachers can better prepare their learners for summative expectations with the productive group work and speaking and listening standards when they clearly know where their learners are *during* the learning. The tenet of instructional agility requires teachers to use emerging evidence. Classroom dialogue provides a primary medium for teachers to hear and clarify student thinking. When teachers generate conversation in formative moments, they are able to observe and hear evidence of student understanding and misunderstanding as it emerges. Finally, students are more able to invest in their learning when they can control for it. When students have an opportunity to participate and frame their own thoughts and beliefs as a result of the discussion at hand, they tend to care more about the overall results and their specific role in shaping those results. These three tenets provide the footing on which teachers build engaging conversations.

The purpose of engineering engaging conversations is to improve learning—the very core of formative assessment work. In order to promote and sustain continued student learning, teachers must thoughtfully consider planning classroom conversations around the following.

- Appropriate topics
- Links to the standards
- Quality criteria for decision making
- Variations of formats for discussion
- Variations of groupings for the students to be successful
- Connections in and among the various assessments used along the learning pathway

In other words, careful assessment planning must go into the work of engineering engaging conversations.

When students are doing all the talking, teachers are more readily available to gather the emerging evidence they require to make instructional decisions and relevant modifications. Gathering evidence midstream is important to a teacher's instructional success. Even when teachers are not using lengthy, engaging conversations to support learning, they can plant key questions—what Dylan Wiliam (2011) calls *hinge questions*—in the middle of a lesson to better hear and understand what students are thinking. When teachers use emerging evidence to isolate simple mistakes, misconceptions, and errors along the way, they can make more informed choices about their next steps. (We explore hinge questions more in depth in chapter 3, page 63.)

Students are more likely to invest in their own learning when engaged in appropriate and meaningful learning conversations for three reasons. First, if the conversation truly is engaging, it piques students' curiosity and interest. Second, learning is more likely to occur when students themselves talk their way into or make meaning around the concepts at hand. And third, the resulting ownership from their personal contributions in the discussion activities can increase motivation for continued learning. Most important, in a learning culture, engaging students in meaningful conversations provides them with the necessary opportunities for intellectual risk taking, productive failure, and celebrated successes (Frey, Fisher, & Everlove, 2009; Wiliam, 2011).

# Engineering Engaging Conversations in Action

Engineering engaging conversations changes the way teachers provide instruction. Conversations provide the guidance students need to think about their own thinking and own their own learning. Following are examples and strategies for promoting engaging conversations in the classroom.

## Two Examples of Instruction

Imagine a team is teaching sixth graders to write an argumentative essay. Of course, such work likely requires an entire unit of study, spanning a few weeks, no matter what type of instruction teachers provide. In a typical, more traditional system, the following pattern of instruction might occur.

- The teacher introduces the concept of argumentative writing.
- The teacher provides an anchor text for the entire class to use to diagnose and name the key components of the argument.

- The teacher provides students with a graphic organizer for argumentation writing.

- Students select or receive a topic, fill in the graphic organizer, and then draft their argument essays.

- Students share their drafts for peer review and editing.

- Students revise and submit their argument essays.

In this system, teachers walk students through the entire process and provide them with tools that—while helpful—do the thinking for them. The resulting evidence (the essay) is more about the students' ability to follow the guidelines than it is about their understanding of how to build arguments and their ability to independently develop effective ones. Moreover, in this instructional sequence, there is likely only enough time to explore one option (one anchor text, one graphic organizer) for argumentation writing, and teachers do not expose students to the variety of options at their disposal for structuring an effective argument.

If a teacher used the process of engaging conversations to navigate the instruction, the process might look more like the following.

- The teacher introduces the concept of argumentative writing and creates interest in and rationale for the importance of argument.

- The teacher provides an anchor text for the entire class to use to diagnose and name the key components of the argument. Students analyze the types of evidence the author uses to construct the argument and begin to identify the types of criteria that determine quality evidence. Together, the class tries to create a graphic organizer or map that shows the relationships of the components and traces the argument in the text.

- The teacher places students into teams (three to six students per team) and provides a new anchor text that uses a different framework to structure the argument. Using a team structure with provided roles and rules, students collaborate to replicate the same process they used as a large group, identifying the parts of the argument, identifying the quality of the evidence used to support the argument, and finally tracing its structure.

- Teams conclude their investigation by developing a graphic organizer that mirrors the pattern in the text.

- The teams regroup as a whole class to compare their criteria for quality evidence as well as their graphic organizers from the second text, finding similarities and differences among their findings and ultimately building the class argument around the final structure.

- Teachers place students into smaller teams (two to three students per team) and provide a third anchor text that uses a different argument structure. The teams repeat the process they used with the second text and again identify the effectiveness of the evidence the author employs. They then create the visual tool that outlines the structure of the third text. Multiple teams share their graphic organizers to discuss their findings and ask the following questions.

  - "What types of evidence are best when trying to convince someone of something? How much evidence is sufficient?"

  - "What are the similarities and differences in the teams' graphic organizers for the third text?"

  - "What are the similarities and differences between the graphic organizers for texts 1, 2, and 3?"

  - "Is one structure better than another? If so, why? If not, why not?"

  - "Does the topic dictate the type of structure that is best to use?"

- Teachers ask students to develop their own argumentative essays. They can select from the graphic organizers the class has already mapped, or they can create their own structures for their arguments.

- Students solicit feedback from their peers on the quality of the evidence they have selected to include in their arguments.

- Students individually draft and submit their argument essays.

In the second example, students co-create meaning about what a quality argument looks like. As a result, they gain a deeper understanding of the overall process of argumentation as well as a strong grasp of the degree of care and intentionality someone must use to create a quality argument. In addition, as the conversations unfold, the teacher has many opportunities to provide feedback to individuals and student teams as they develop their understanding of argumentation. These types of structured conversations set up opportunities for teachers to be instructionally agile in targeted ways.

It might seem like the second example would take too much time. However, consider table 2.1 (page 40) for ways to create the space to accomplish such work.

*Table 2.1: Benefits and Options for Streamlining Engaging Conversations*

| Benefits for Students of Engineering Engaging Conversations | Options for Teachers to Streamline Content and Create Space for Engaging Conversations |
|---|---|
| <ul><li>Experience increased rigor.</li><li>Learn how to make informed decisions with quality options.</li><li>Explore multiple structures for argumentation.</li><li>Study broader perspectives on options for developing arguments.</li><li>Improve their use of evidence for future arguments in writing, speeches, or debates.</li><li>Experience productive group work.</li><li>Work with varied group sizes and different members within groups.</li><li>Receive individual and group feedback during instruction to maximize instructional time.</li></ul> | <ul><li>Integrate multiple standards to accomplish more in an abbreviated time frame.</li><li>If elementary or secondary interdisciplinary, draw texts from multiple disciplines (for example, science, social studies, art) to cover relevant content from other curricular areas.</li><li>If secondary, draw texts that include information about required content for upcoming units of study so the investigation helps jumpstart student understanding.</li><li>Reduce the number of traditional pencil-and-paper assessments or the amount of content covered to create space for more in-depth reasoning and collaboration.</li><li>Provide feedback as the conversations unfold, and target individuals and student teams more intentionally (and with more impact on achievement) as students engage in conversations. This can reduce the number of written comments, which students often ignore, and time outside of class.</li></ul> |

When teachers take the time to build a firm foundation for content and process and teach students how to learn along the way, they are likely to accelerate the pace of learning as the year progresses; a front-end investment yields a back-end payoff.

Engineering conversations requires considerable planning and attention to the assessment architecture in advance of employing the strategy. At the outset, it's important for teachers to consider how they integrate the standards and disciplines involved, the learning targets for the standards they will measure, and the time required to accomplish those tasks. An engaging conversation can involve a single class period (for example, take an author's stance to argue a key question, analyze common errors in student work, or peer-edit student work), an extended period over several days, or even an entire semester (for example, research and frame a debate, explore an issue to identify the problem and its variables, or generate a solution to a complex problem). It's equally important to maintain a sense of the big picture of engineering engaging conversations over time, given that students need varied group members, discussion formats, rules, and roles if they are to receive full exposure to speaking and listening standards and productive group work experiences.

Ultimately, engineering conversations is about designing quality performance assessments. This means teachers predesign worthy questions and tasks with clear guidelines for the criteria to be measured (generated from standards and learning targets) and how they will measure them (for example, rubrics, checklists, or timing) to set up the best possible conditions for students to succeed. Worthy questions and prompts include the following.

- **Intriguing or interesting:** The question, prompt, or task piques curiosity. (For example, when making an argument for one side of an issue, is it more effective to use your strongest point first or last?)

- **Relevant:** The question, prompt, or task matters to students in the here and now; it has a compelling and clear connection to their learning now and in the future. (For example, is heat or ice the more effective remedy for a pulled hamstring?)

- **Complex:** The tasks ask students to develop new conclusions, make connections, synthesize ideas, and critically and creatively problem solve. They cannot base their conclusions solely on right or wrong answers. There is more than one solution or response to the task. (For example, should our city invest in expanded freeways or expanded rapid transit?)

- **Worthy:** The resulting answers or solutions lead to valuable discoveries, insights, knowledge, and skills that promote continued learning. (For example, in what ways did each of your strengths uniquely contribute to the success of your team discussion?)

A well-designed question, prompt, or task can make all the difference as to whether students spend considerable amounts of time engaging in collective inquiry and problem solving.

## Productive Group Work

Teachers should place students in groups intentionally "because when learners are away from the teacher, they rely on one another to be successful" (Fisher & Frey, 2010, p. 118). A student's group can enhance or inhibit his or her individual learning and temper the quality of his or her experience. Research indicates that homogeneous or ability grouping—especially when sustained for long periods of time—can have a very negative effect (Hattie, 2009). With sustained homogeneous grouping, the gap between the haves and the have-nots widens, bankrupting the classroom culture required to support intellectual risk taking by all students.

Teaching students the skills of productive group work and ensuring a culture of safety and support create an environment conducive to success. Teachers must consider particular student variables, such as attitudes, interests, prior knowledge, readiness, language, cultural background, personal strengths and stretches, and rate of learning, to name a few, when forming groups. Heterogeneous groups have advantages when students engage in collective inquiry because the variety of students involved can provide opportunities for modeling, which offers them exposure to alternative ways to think and act when they engage in productive group work. Within heterogeneous groups, it's important to establish guidelines and protocols to maintain the goal that all students contribute in similar ways to the group effort; this ensures that more proficient students don't dominate the experience.

Students will participate in a variety of groups over time in any given course and throughout their academic careers. It is even possible that they will take an active role in multiple groups at a single point in time. A student may have a long-standing peer-editing partner with whom he or she meets once a week but a different small group for a specific task in each new unit of instruction. Both the structure of the discussion format and the content of the task impact the decisions regarding who belongs in which group. For example, some discussion formats, like philosophical chairs, peer review, or think-pair-share, are one on one, while other formats, like debate, Socratic seminar, or literature circles, often involve significantly larger groups.

The purpose or focus of collaborative work also dictates how teachers compose groups. The group a student needs for collective inquiry will be different than the group for brainstorming, arguing, reviewing, and so on. Given the desired outcome, teachers would need to decide if the range of student proficiency in a group's composition would be more or less advantageous to the students involved. According to Erkens (2015), these are some of the groups students might encounter within a single classroom.

- **A = Assigned (teacher discretion based on reteaching and intervention needs):** Teachers assign these groups after making students aware of which learning targets they are going to address through more focused efforts. It is a data-driven decision, and students have their own data to support various learning needs. In the A grouping, students may engage in error analysis, review content or processes, participate in extensions or enrichments, and so on. The assigned groupings change after each significant assessment that involves interventions or enrichments.

- **B = Buddy (student choice, but teachers encourage students to find different buddies throughout the term):** On B days, students engage in brainstorming, discussion, reflection activities, and so on. This is a generative and play-based grouping when the stakes are low and when the teacher wants to stimulate fun and creativity. This works well when exploring or introducing a topic in which teachers develop student understanding of the relevance and interest or intrigue in the topic of study.

- **C = Collaborative project (teacher assembles mixed-ability groups of three to five students for two- to six-week collaborative projects):** The letter C is on the board when collaboration is a focal point so learning activities are very structured and ultimately assessed. The groupings are intentional by either mixed or like abilities. Social learning happens when the teacher outlines specific stretch activities scaffolded by student readiness and interest so all group members contribute to the outcome.

- **D = Design and destination work (teacher identifies two to three peers of like abilities to work together on feedback and goal-setting activities):** Such groupings allow teachers the opportunity to differentiate as they move in and among the various groupings based on students' self-identified but evidence-based goals. Unlike A groups, which are based on needs after a specific assessment, D groups are based on long-term goals for which students have input. Teachers form D groups after students have established their goals. Students work together to engage in practice, error analysis, peer review, reflection, goal setting, discussion of concerns and needs, progress tracking against specific learning expectations, and so on.

- **E = Everyone (whole-group work for instruction, discussion, debate, setting criteria, collaborative scoring, error analysis, practicing feedback, and so on):** When E is on the board, students know they will still have a high level of collaborative interaction as the teacher navigates whole-group discussion using accountability strategies that keep everyone engaged with full participation.

No matter the selected structure, teachers cannot leave the work of collaboration to chance. Preplanning and careful consideration are necessary to engineer engaging conversations in the classroom.

Teachers must instruct students on the skills of productive group work. Once students learn these skills, they need to practice them regularly under teacher observation and monitoring. It's not natural for all students to navigate a learning conversation, especially if they have no previous experience operating that way. To support such a dramatic shift in the learning process, teachers need to spend instructional time establishing the guidelines, protocols, discussion formats, rules and roles, and the language of academic transitions. Students must learn how to engage in learning conversations.

# Strategies and Tools

To successfully engineer engaging conversations, teachers must be strategic, preparing learners the right way and covering the gamut of expectations required for productive group work. The following strategies and the tools provided within each can support their efforts in truly engineering powerful conversations.

- **Strategy 1:** Clarify expectations for learning conversations
- **Strategy 2:** Vary discussion formats, rules, and roles
- **Strategy 3:** Teach the language of engaging conversations
- **Strategy 4:** Monitor individual and group effectiveness
- **Strategy 5:** Monitor conversation effectiveness

## Strategy 1: Clarify Expectations for Learning Conversations

While conversations might seem commonplace, the truth is that navigating productive discourse poses a challenge. Learners must first understand what quality conversation looks like. An important first step involves engaging students in observing quality examples and nonexamples of learning conversations so they can isolate the criteria and measuring tools for their own work. According to renowned assessment experts, the most powerful formative assessment strategy a teacher can use is to make the learning expectations visible (Chappuis, 2014; Hattie, 2009, 2012; Wiliam, 2011).

Learning expectations come in the form of learning targets (*what* students need to know from the standards) and quality criteria for the performance of those standards (*how good is good enough*). Students need to see and understand both in order to succeed. Yet another powerful formative assessment strategy involves looking at samples of strong and weak work as a means to help students understand the quality expectations (Chappuis, 2014). They must see and understand what teachers are asking them to do so they can self-monitor their own effectiveness.

Figure 2.1 provides the protocol for examining strong and weak examples of student-engaged learning conversations to clarify expectations for quality learning experiences. The protocol takes several days initially because of the time required to view and discuss videos and gather large-group input. But a single swipe at rehearsal will not suffice. Teachers who generate amazing results with engaging conversations make this work an ongoing study for continual improvement. They can engage the class in role playing, observing, sharing feedback, evaluating, and even self- and team evaluating during the actual performances. In other words, the protocol we outline in figure 2.1 never really ends. It is through these moments of role playing, observing, feedback, and self-evaluation that teachers intentionally recognize where students are in their understanding of any targeted learning expectations (standard, learning target, or success criteria). These moments provide opportunities for teachers to offer verbal feedback and in-the-moment opportunities for students to apply that feedback. Teachers interpret students' words and actions (or lack of them), which makes engineering engaging conversations a powerful moment for teachers to be instructionally agile. It's also entirely possible to employ these strategies without intention, and miss that powerful moment.

| Step | Task | Resources Needed |
|------|------|------------------|
| 1 | Begin by identifying desired criteria for a quality collaborative learning conversation. Knowing the criteria in advance can help you select video samples. | English language arts standards that support engaging conversations: <br> • Speaking and listening <br> • Reading (text evidence) <br> • Writing (argumentation) |
| 2 | Find age- and topic-appropriate video samples of students engaged in learning-based discourse. Seek examples that provide direct evidence of the identified criteria from step 1. <br><br> Isolate segments that are three to ten minutes in length (shorter for elementary students) to tease out key concepts. | Predetermined criteria for quality <br><br> Video library or websites with appropriate videos (for example, EngageNY; TeachingChannel .org, YouTube) |
| 3 | Engage students in discovery learning as they watch the preplanned videos. <br><br> Ask students what they notice about the conversation. Have teams of students discuss their observations before bringing the conversation to the large group. Share the important questions for students to discuss (see the following questions). <br><br> Facilitate a large-group conversation to highlight student responses to the following important questions. <br> • What are the students in the conversation doing? <br> • How are they behaving? <br> • How are they talking? <br> • What are they not doing? <br><br> Use questions and cues to help students isolate the desired criteria. <br><br> Record the criteria as they emerge. | Video equipment and sound system <br><br> Space to record student observations <br><br> Chart that lists all the student names in the class to document moments of deep understanding and misconceptions to address in the moment or later on |

***Figure 2.1: Protocol for examining samples of strong and weak student conversations.***

continued ➔

| Step | Task | Resources Needed |
|------|------|------------------|
| 4 | Develop an array of monitoring tools with the class using the class-identified criteria. Engage teams in collective brainstorming before engaging in whole-class discussion.<br><br>For example, you might say, "We said using academic transitions was an important part of a good learning conversation. How could we track and monitor our ability to use academic transitions?"<br><br>Students might respond, "We could have someone observe our conversation and record all of the academic transitions they hear us use from our anchor chart. They could tally words that we use more than once, and we could even see if we could find new words to add to the anchor chart."<br><br>Ask students to consider the following types of tools.<br><br>• **Tracking forms:** One for monitoring each key feature (for example, number of academic transitions, number of times someone paraphrases, number of quotes used, number of citations offered, number of questions asked)<br><br>• **Big board tracking:** For monitoring and recording the flow of the discussion<br><br>• **Student data-tracking forms:** For monitoring data regarding an individual's performance against given criteria that students track and use for decision making during a conversation or goal setting between conversations<br><br>• **Peer coach forms:** When students partner with someone for half-time feedback, which is provided halfway through the process so the student can improve the performance's second half<br><br>• **Feedback forms for reflecting following a learning discussion:**<br>  • Team forms<br>  • Self-reflection forms<br>  • Other monitoring tools as defined by the students and linked to the criteria<br><br>Once the teams generate ideas for the criteria to track, engage them in designing the tools to help with tracking. (For example, one team develops a team reflection and student reflection form, and another team designs the data trackers for tallying observations.)<br><br>Teams share tools for review, revision, and final approval for the whole class to use. | You may use these monitoring tools to identify the type of feedback each student can act on to improve his or her learning. |

| 5 | Role-play group discussions in a fishbowl setting, with students on the outer circle gathering the predetermined data using the new data-gathering forms. | An engaging conversation prompt or task |
|---|---|---|
| | Facilitate a large-group debrief. Share the data gathered and ask the class to reflect on the effectiveness of the collaborative conversation. What worked? What could be better? | Student-created data-gathering forms |
| | Repeat this process as often as needed (over the course of time) to cover new discussion-based skills and processes as teachers introduce them. | |
| | • New collaborative formats (for example, Socratic seminar, pinwheel dialogue, or debate) | |
| | • New roles (for example, process analyst or spokesperson) or rules (for example, team norms) | |
| | • New challenges or considerations for teams (for example, how to get to consensus or how to navigate conflict) | |
| 6 | Organize teams and launch collaborative conversations. | Use the sources that were created in step 4 during the conversations. |
| | • Vary the discussion formats used over time (see strategy 2). | |
| | • Vary the size of groups over time. | |
| | • Vary the members of groups over time. | |
| | • Engage students in data tracking during all the discussions. | |
| | • Engage students in reflection every time—self, team, and whole class. Identify next steps for future conversations. | |

Table 2.2 (page 48) outlines possible learning targets from the Common Core Speaking and Listening standards. Of course, teachers must write learning targets in student-friendly language, so the samples would change to accommodate the age of the students involved. We intend the targets we list to accomplish the following.

- Use instruction to engage learners in talking about learning by collaboratively examining samples of strong and weak work—their own and others'.

- Keep students focused on the few things that matter most.

- Provide key features that are generalizable enough that students may track them over time.

- Create generalizable constructs that students can employ no matter the structure of the selected discussion formats.

***Table 2.2:*** *Sample Learning Targets and Quality Criteria for Evaluation*

| Learning Targets (Based on Common Core Speaking and Listening Standards) | Criteria |
|---|---|
| I can exchange ideas. This means I can ask and answer questions or offer statements so I am contributing to the conversation. | • Offers genuine, thoughtful questions as a mechanism to explore someone else's contribution or to elicit information from a group member<br>• Responds directly to the questions asked with clear and concise answers<br>• Prompts continued civil discourse with open-minded, logical answers<br>• Shares personal beliefs and ideas in a respectful and inviting way to welcome input from others |
| I can reference my background preparation during a conversation. This means I gather information in advance of the discussion by reading, viewing, and listening, and then I quote, paraphrase, or reference exact sources to support my own ideas when I am talking. | • Uses evidence from background materials to rationalize personal thoughts and contributions<br>• Easily and readily employs quotes and paraphrases from reference materials to support claims<br>• Locates appropriate references to respond to questions or statements from peers |
| I can keep a conversation moving forward. This means I can propel a conversation and help a group maintain the focus of a conversation. | • Adds contributions with the intent of igniting new ideas or next steps<br>• Uses academic transitions to navigate the flow of the conversation and link disparate ideas<br>• Employs redirection strategies or cues when the conversation drifts off topic<br>• Guarantees that all members are on task and have addressed key points |
| I can follow the structures and guidelines of any discussion format. This means I can employ agreed-upon rules and adopt the necessary roles to make the conversation run smoothly. | • Uses the rules of the selected discussion structure to support healthy dialogue among all team members<br>• Employs the assigned role to help facilitate the work of the team<br>• Monitors self and others for adhering to the rules and roles of discourse |

The table also offers a set of plausible criteria (again, these would need to be age appropriate and specifically tied to the standards for that grade level) that a teacher could use as a guide to facilitate conversations with students on what matters most when examining strong and weak examples of collaborative learning conversations. The criteria are also a guide for teachers to focus their individual feedback on students to improve their engagement in the conversation and to nurture their proficiency in whatever standard is at hand.

## Strategy 2: Vary Discussion Formats, Rules, and Roles

Almost all speaking and listening standards (Common Core or individual state or province standards) require students to engage in a variety of *all* of the following.

- Discussion formats

- Group sizes

- Partners (for example, with individuals older, younger, of like mind, or of alternative perspectives)

- Topics that are age appropriate

For example, the grade 4 Common Core Speaking and Listening standard reads: "Engage effectively in a range of collaborative discussions (one-on-one, in groups, teacher-led) with diverse partners on grade 4 topics and texts, building on others' ideas and expressing their own clearly" (SL.4.11; NGA & CCSSO, 2010). The standards also suggest that students follow a wide array of agreed-upon rules to use the selected format for the discussion and carry out assigned roles.

Table 2.3 provides a working list of potential discussion formats teachers could use to support the work of varying collaborative conversation formats, rules, and roles.

**Table 2.3:** *Structures to Support Engineering Engaging Conversations*

| Discussion Format | Description |
|---|---|
| **Show and Tell** | A student or students shows something to the audience and then shares detailed information, related experiences, or personal insights about the item. |
| **Think-Pair-Share (or Think-Pair-Square)** | Small teams of students work together to answer a question or respond to a prompt. In the process, students must (1) think individually about a topic or answer to a question; (2) pair with others; and (3) share ideas in pairs (two students) or squares (four students). Teachers can assign various requirements (such as coming to consensus or finding the most common answer to share) to the final pairing before they report back to the whole group. |

continued →

| Discussion Format | Description |
|---|---|
| **Philosophical Chairs** | Students receive a central topic or question with which they must agree, disagree, or be neutral in their response. They explore new information in advance of a class discussion and then join a semicircle arrangement of chairs to argue the merits of a philosophical question or prompt. |
| **Hot Seat** | A student adopts the persona of a character, historian, or scientist and then (from the hot seat at the front of the room) answers class questions from the perspective of that character about the historical event or scientific investigation. |
| **Mathematics Talks** | The whole group or small teams of students engage in mathematics-specific learning conversations during which they explore various solutions, examine processes for arriving at those solutions, challenge thinking, and ultimately construct new knowledge or deeper conceptual understanding of the mathematical process. |
| **Juried Forums** | Teams of students work in a court-like or tribunal meeting structure. Teachers assign each team a perspective, and team members engage in using text evidence to defend a position. Each team adopts a separate perspective (unlike debate, which is often limited to a pro-or-con approach) regarding a central issue. To begin, a team must state and defend its position using solid evidence, and then respond extemporaneously to inquiries from other teams, who ask clarifying questions and challenge the premise of the presenting team. The goal is to win the argument with the most compelling stance and supporting evidence for both the statement of the initial position and the extemporaneously offered, text-based responses. |
| **Debate** | Students engage in a formal discussion on a particular topic in a public meeting or legislative assembly, in which they present opposing arguments. Students must engage in significant research in advance of the discussion and follow specific rules of conduct throughout the ensuing conversation. |
| **Socratic Seminar** | A circle of students engages in a formal discussion based on a text. They respond to open-ended questions that participating students generate and pose, listen closely to the comments of others, analyze responses, and articulate their own thoughts. In an optional twist, an outer circle of students may monitor the conversation for evidence of effectiveness (number of points made, quality of conversation, number of times individuals speak, and so on). The outer ring may operate as a source of feedback or coach to inner-ring participants midway through the dialogue. |
| **Literature Circles** | Small groups of students gather together to discuss a piece of literature in depth. Students' responses to what they have read guide the discussion. Questions and comments may center on understanding the passage to interpret, draw conclusions, or make connections to other texts or events. |

| POGIL (Process-Oriented Guided Inquiry Learning) | Students operate in a guided inquiry approach most often through a science-related experience. POGIL is an acronym for process-oriented guided inquiry learning. Formal processes guide students through a learning cycle of exploration, concept invention, and application as the basis for many of the carefully designed materials students use to guide them to construct new knowledge. |
|---|---|
| Pinwheel Dialogues | The teacher divides the class into smaller teams of "text experts" who take responsibility for a primary text and then work to answer key questions as their assigned author might. They use text evidence to back their assertions. Only one student at a time can be in the hot seat, and teams can tap out (tap the speaker's shoulder and replace him or her in the dialogue) of the hot seat as desired or needed. Small groups continue to rotate individual team members (tied to their specific text) in a pinwheel fashion, making sure everyone has the opportunity to be in the center dialogue, where all the various texts are being connected to each other (Brown Wessling, n.d.). |

Each format offers its own set of rules and roles. Once the teacher selects a format, he or she finds the specifics regarding the rules of that particular conversation construct; or in some cases, where information is slim, creates the rules that help students succeed. We list common roles in table 2.4. Note, however, that not all roles apply to all discussion formats. Teachers and students must identify the best or most appropriate roles, determined by the construct of the conversation and the demands of the group's assigned task. Some roles are directly within the team (facilitator, reporter); others are within the circle of observers (peer coach, scribe); and still others might be inside or outside the team itself (time keeper, process analyst). Sometimes, multiple students might engage in the same role, such as the process analysts and peer coaches. A single conversation will not employ all the roles, so teachers will want to decide in advance which roles work best for the structure and purpose of the conversation.

## Table 2.4: Common Roles in a Collaborative Discussion

| Common Roles | Description |
|---|---|
| Facilitator | The role of the facilitator is to enable people and processes to be successful in any given meeting, encouraging the group to discover or create their own solutions. |
| Note Taker | Unlike the recorder, the note taker simply documents all the salient points to remember. However, it's important that group members keep their own notes so they have their own record to reference for future needs. This way, they are independently accountable for the learning and cannot defer to someone else to engage in capturing the essence for them. |

continued ➡

| Common Roles | Description |
|---|---|
| **Recorder** | The role of the recorder is to document the results of the meeting in formal notes that all attendees receive following the conclusion of the meeting. A recorder creates a record of actions and decisions. |
| **Scribe or Big Board Recorder** | The role of the scribe is to create a visual representation of the group's discussion or decisions on whiteboards or flip charts at the front of the room, helping the group remain focused on the key points of discussion. |
| **Reporter or Spokesperson** | The reporter or spokesperson speaks for his or her team when engaging with the large group to reflect team conversation. Reporters serve as the conduit to the larger group, asking questions, seeking input, and offering the conclusions of their group. They can always confer with their team for a moment before responding to a large-group prompt, especially when another team challenges them in the moment. |
| **Process Observer** | The role of the process observer is one of objective reflection or feedback to the group. This assumes that the group would like to look at its behavior objectively and improve upon it. The process observer may be a member of the small group who steps outside the process to record the data the team has asked him or her to gather. Or, the observer can be any other respected person whom the team has asked to observe it, record requested information, and provide feedback. |
| **Process Analyst** | Process analysts monitor the key processes worth tracking. They can operate within the team, giving feedback at strategic moments, or they can operate outside the team, tracking the key skills (for example, asking questions, answering questions, using academic transitions) and sharing their data findings at the conclusion of the meeting for the class to analyze results and strategize next steps. There may be more than one process analyst in a conversation, with each one monitoring something specific. |
| **Quality Controller** | The quality controller gathers evidence of the overall effectiveness of the conversation. Is it on point? Focused? Inclusive of background preparation? Does it generate new insights and meaning? Is learning occurring? Quality controllers may be internal or external to a team's discussion. Their feedback should improve the overall quality of the learning portion of the conversations at hand. |
| **Peer Coach** | The peer coach is helpful for lengthy conversations, such as the Socratic seminar. Peer coaches observe, gather data of effectiveness, and then provide feedback and coaching to their assigned partners who are operating within the conversation. Their half-time feedback should set up their partners to improve their own results with data-based recommendations for next steps in the second half of the ongoing conversation. |

| Time Keeper | The role of the time keeper is to keep the group on track regarding allocated times for the meeting's beginning and ending and key discussions throughout. The time keeper notifies the facilitator when time is nearly up, allowing the facilitator to engage the participants in problem solving if they will not complete the discussion the time provided. |
|---|---|

It is helpful to provide or co-create with students cue cards that define the roles in the early stages of practicing conversations that require the identified roles.

## Strategy 3: Teach the Language of Engaging Conversations

Students who have limited experience with engaging conversations can be very uncomfortable with sharing a role in the dialogue. Providing them with the necessary constructs can increase their confidence levels. Students need the language of academic transitions and stems they can use to connect ideas during a discussion.

Many students lack the academic vocabulary they need to navigate text or media. A considerable feature of the Common Core State Standards involves helping students acquire academic vocabulary, specifically the language of transitions, which students can use to show the relationship between and among the ideas they discuss. Figure 2.2 outlines the types of vocabulary transition terms students need to succeed in engaging conversations. It can also be helpful to create anchor charts or desk-sized cue cards to help students in the early stages of connecting ideas during a discussion.

| | | |
|---|---|---|
| As a result | Therefore | Similarly |
| As well as | Furthermore | Additionally |
| However | In the first place | In conclusion |
| Likewise | On a similar note | As a consequence |
| On the other hand | Regardless | Nonetheless |
| Instead | Despite | Although |
| On the contrary | Then again | In contrast |
| Consequently | Accordingly | With this in mind |
| Generally | Alternately | Specifically |

*Figure 2.2: Academic transitions.*

Speaking and listening standards require that students initiate conversations, stay on point during a conversation, and ask and answer questions throughout the conversation. The standards also require that students reference their background preparation of text or media sources. Students may need scaffolding as they start out. They must understand the types of sentence leads they could use when quoting, paraphrasing, inviting, probing, or initiating. They should also practice sample stems until they can operate independently as they interact with each other. Figure 2.3 outlines the types of possible sentence stems teachers can consider when building anchor charts or desk cue cards with students.

---

### Quoting

- "According to (name of author), _____ (provide exact words)."
- "In the (book, article, or text) _____ (name passage), the author says _____ (provide exact words)." (Try other strong action verbs to replace *said* or *says*; try options like *adds, argues, writes, declares, notes, suggests, replies, states*, or *remarks*.)
- "The author (provide name) proclaims, (provide exact words); this means _____ (provide your interpretation)."

### Paraphrasing

- "The author (provide name) is trying to say _____ (highlight key message)."
- "The main idea or theme of the text is that _____ (highlight key message)."
- "I think you are suggesting _____ (highlight key message)."
- "Your idea that _____ (highlight key message), is . . . (add your own thoughts)."

### Inviting

- "What are your thoughts about this, _____ (name of participant)?"
- "Are there any additional ideas that we have not explored yet?"
- "I wonder if we've heard from everyone. Would anyone else like to share?"
- "I agree with what you are saying. Can you add any supporting details?"

### Probing

- "Can you help me understand what you meant when you said _____ (plug in participant's words)?"
- "Can you back that idea with any text? What or who are you referencing when you make that statement?"
- "Can you say that in another way? I'm not sure I understand."
- "Let's talk about that a little more. I have another thought that's a little different (share thought)."
- "I disagree because _____ (share thought). Can you clarify your ideas further so I can better understand?"
- "I'm wondering about _____ (share thought)."

---

**Initiating**

- "To get started, let's _____ (fill in next steps)."
- "Let's begin by _____ (fill in first step)."
- "I believe _____ (share belief). What do others think?"
- "I'm excited, curious, or wondering about _____ (fill in idea). Can we talk about that?"
- "Let's take this conversation in another direction. We haven't yet discussed _____ (fill in topic that's related to overall conversation)."

---

*Figure 2.3: Sample student speaking and listening stems.*

A student's success in this area is less about what the teacher posts on the walls to read and more about *how* and *when* the teacher co-creates the anchor materials with the class.

## Strategy 4: Monitor Individual and Group Effectiveness

It can be impossible to watch and listen to every single student when multiple conversations are happening at once. Find ways to strategically gather evidence of effectiveness so feedback can effectively move individuals and groups of students forward in their proficiency. The following options can make the process more manageable.

- Organize teams in such a way that external observers are available, and then engage observers in gathering data that they document, discuss, and turn in as companion data to support observations.

- Randomly select students or teams to observe at a given point in time, making sure each team or student has your attention at various points. Create multiple prompts so those engaged in conversations have a fresh topic linked to the standards they are exploring but that does not inspire them to simply regurgitate the discussion they previously observed. For example, create two debate topics so group A's topic is different than group B's, but both link to the standards the groups are discussing.

- Engage the teams in reflecting on and recording their own effectiveness. Require students to use evidence to back their evaluations. Use this evidence as a companion feature and not a replacement of your professional judgment. And, use the evidence to help students set goals for future improvement in the key skills.

## *Strategy 5: Monitor Conversation Effectiveness*

Not every task is a guaranteed success. In this case, use the opportunity to learn what works and what does not by engaging in action research regarding the effectiveness of the engineered conversations. Were the tasks meaningful? Were the prompts provocative? Did quality work emerge as a result? Engineering engaging conversations allows teachers the opportunity to observe the effectiveness of the question or task as well as individual and group proficiency.

First, it's important to know what criteria to use to determine if a question or task was productive. The three criteria—engagement, learning, and collaboration—that figure 2.4 outlines can help students initiate the conversation with peers on what to notice when monitoring engaging conversations.

| Engagement | **Student Participation** |
|---|---|
| | Almost all students, almost all of the time, verbally engage in the high-cognitive-demand tasks that teachers pose during the conversation. |
| | Students demonstrate that they can participate in and show an evolving understanding of the targeted learning. The teacher can assess, interpret, and push students' level of proficiency through engagement in this task. |
| | Students sustain all conversations at a high level of challenge and application. |
| | **The Task** |
| | The teacher plans the task at a high level of cognitive reasoning (assess, revise, critique, draw conclusions, differentiate, formulate, hypothesize, and cite evidence). |
| | The task requires students to investigate, which requires time to think and process multiple conditions of the problem (synthesize, analyze, prove, connect, design, and apply concepts). |
| Learning | **Student Participation** |
| | Through participating in engaging conversations, students learn and grow effective in their talk. |
| | Students challenge each other's thinking, extend current thinking, and create new possibilities. |
| | The conversation involves sharing ideas, and one party (as in the teacher, leader, or coach) does not completely script or control it. |
| | Students recognize the connections between and among concepts and skills. |
| | Students effectively provide formal and informal peer feedback in the moment that aligns with teacher's, leader's, or coach's expectations and clarifies gaps in understanding, misconceptions in concepts, or errors in reasoning. |

| | The meaning and significance of the ideas students generate are compelling enough to influence a larger audience beyond their team (for example, communicating knowledge to others, including within the classroom or school; advocating solutions to social problems; providing assistance to people; or creating performances or products that make a contribution to the greater good).<br><br>**The Task**<br>The task is focused on disciplined inquiry, promotes rich dialogue, and demands active discussion and debate. |
|---|---|
| **Collaboration** | **Student Participation**<br>Students engage in productive, collaborative group work. Group members activate each other as resources. They synergize, capitalize on and strategize, or accommodate for each other's strengths and weaknesses.<br><br>The team follows the rules and roles of the structured dialogue. Students hold each other accountable for following the norms and completing the tasks in a timely manner. The dialogue references background preparation. Members cite and quote or paraphrase to support their individual contributions. The conversation remains focused and oriented toward decision making, problem solving, or designing as a means to complete the task.<br><br>Members build coherently on others' ideas to promote improved collective understanding of a theme or topic. Students expand their collective insights and repertoires of skills and strategies to address errors and gaps in understanding. Students establish a social norm of excellence for all relying on social pressure and collective support to motivate and encourage all students to achieve mastery.<br><br>**The Task**<br>The task requires learners to collaborate and become interdependent. The team designs and produces their collective efforts, and members hold each other accountable to the outcome. In addition, when the task is designed with great care, students learn communication strategies, productive work skills, conflict resolution skills, and ways to assign work and roles so everyone is successful. |

*Figure 2.4: Criteria for monitoring the effectiveness of engaging conversations.*

Once teachers identify the preferred criteria and accommodating descriptions, they can use simple forms to track progress. When tracking the effectiveness of a provocative question during a single class period, a teacher might consider using or modifying the simple form we outline in figure 2.5 (page 58).

| The Question: | | | | | | | | | | | |
|---|---|---|---|---|---|---|---|---|---|---|---|
| Evidence of Engagement: | | | | Evidence of Learning: | | | | Evidence of Collaborating: | | | |
| **Circle the score to match evidence provided (4 is high).** | | | | | | | | | | | |
| 1 | 2 | 3 | 4 | 1 | 2 | 3 | 4 | 1 | 2 | 3 | 4 |

**Reflection:**

What did I learn about questioning as students engaged in answering this question?

Did I have to rephrase or clarify the original question? If so, how?

What did students do with the original question? What types of questions did they ask?

What changes would I make in that lesson in the future?

**Figure 2.5:** *Action research form to monitor effectiveness of quality questions.*

*Visit go.SolutionTree.com/assessment for a free reproducible version of this figure.*

When tracking the effectiveness of a larger task that will likely consume many class periods, a teacher might consider using or modifying the form in figure 2.6. We recommend that teams consist of three to six members for large-group tasks. Smaller numbers empower all students to participate in a sustained conversation. When there are many different teams, consider randomizing which team you observe, and ensure you observe it carefully several times throughout the duration of the task. It is not always necessary to let teams know who you are observing each day.

| **Overview of Task for All Teams** | |
|---|---|
| Unit: | Name of Task: |
| Standard or Standards: | Learning Targets: |
| Duration of Task _____ (estimate number of days) | From _____ to _____ |
| Number of Teams and Team Members (list names in the spaces provided): | |

| Team 1 | Team 2 | Team 3 | Team 4 | Team 5 |
|--------|--------|--------|--------|--------|
|        |        |        |        |        |
|        |        |        |        |        |
|        |        |        |        |        |
|        |        |        |        |        |
|        |        |        |        |        |
|        |        |        |        |        |

| Team Name:<br>Team Members: | | Teacher Notes About Team (for example, membership changes, behavior concerns, instructional interventions): | |
|---|---|---|---|---|
| Dates Observed:<br>_____<br>_____<br>_____<br>_____<br>_____<br>_____<br>_____<br>_____ | Evidence of Engagement: | Evidence of Learning: | Evidence of Collaboration:<br>1.<br><br>2.<br><br>3.<br><br>4. | Overall Score Based on Combined Evidence: |

***Figure 2.6:*** *Action research form to monitor effectiveness of quality tasks.*

*Visit **go.SolutionTree.com/assessment** for a free reproducible version of this figure.*

Teachers can use figure 2.7 (page 60) to monitor individual students for engagement in the conversation and his or her understanding of the content.

| Student Name: | I can come prepared. I will read and research in advance of the discussion, and I will show my preparedness by citing the evidence that I encountered when I was preparing. | I can follow the identified rules. They will guide our discussion, and I can use the role I have been assigned to help the conversation remain on track. | I can exchange ideas. I can build on the ideas others offer by using their words or paraphrasing their ideas before adding my own. When adding my ideas, I can qualify what I mean and justify accuracy by using the evidence from outside sources to show that I am connected to the quality work of other experts. | I can propel and maintain focus during a conversation. I can pose questions and respond to others in a way that invites the conversation to continue or go deeper, but always stay on topic. |
|---|---|---|---|---|

**Figure 2.7:** *Teacher tracking form for monitoring student engagement and comprehension.*

Visit **go.SolutionTree.com/assessment** for a free reproducible version of this figure.

# Conclusion

Engineering engaging conversations serves two important purposes within instructional agility: (1) students gain deeper understanding when they talk about what they are learning and (2) teachers gain deeper insight into students' thinking, which provides them more accurate information to interpret and help them make agile maneuvers within instruction. Teachers must use a lot of instructional time teaching the process in order to maximize these two purposes. It might feel like a loss of invaluable teaching time; however, when students control the learning within the parameters of carefully designed tasks, the gains are astounding.

Students can go further in the curriculum than they may have in previous years, and their depth of understanding is profound. These types of engineered conversations provide in-the-moment evidence of where students are in achieving essential learning outcomes. As teachers recognize where students are in their learning, they can more effectively make instructional moves to capitalize and push them to achieve at higher levels. It may take time to perfect the process of engaging students in meaningful, sustained learning conversations, but it is only when this begins to happen that classrooms become places where students are finally working as hard if not harder than their teachers.

# Pause and Ponder

Take a few moments to reflect on the following questions.

- Address the following questions in terms of what is most common in your classroom.

  - Are students interested and engaged? Can they articulate the relevance of what they are learning?

  - Are students retaining information long after you conduct summative assessments?

  - Are students activating each other as resources? Are they working hard alongside you (and other teachers) in the classroom?

  - Are students sharing the responsibility of helping everyone achieve at high levels?

  - Are students making significant connections? Are they challenging each other's understanding?

  - Do students understand how to collaborate in meaningful and productive ways?

- For the questions to which you answered *no* or *not to the fullest potential,* how could you use the structures, ideas, and notions of engineering engaging conversations to improve that outcome?

- How are you using conversations to gather evidence and make instructional moves to push students to higher levels of achievement?

- How are you using or could you engineer engaging conversations to provide formative feedback that students could use to grow and learn more?

# CHAPTER 3
# QUESTIONING

*Questions wake people up. They prompt new ideas. They show people new places, new ways of doing things.*

—Michael Marquardt

Questions generate curiosity, promote engagement, provide insight into how students make sense of things, and lead to interesting new ideas and potentially innovative solutions to persisting problems. In his book *A More Beautiful Question*, Warren Berger (2014) makes a compelling case for the role questioning plays in providing meaningful solutions to pressing dilemmas.

Among many examples across disciplines and situations, he describes the plight of Van Phillips, a bright and athletic college student who lost his left foot in a boating accident in 1976. Upon waking up and realizing his new reality, he heard from many people that he would just have to get used to it. The doctors fit him with a wooden foot and assured him if he walked through the pain, his leg would toughen up and become more comfortable. Phillips, however, was not satisfied with that reality. He wondered, "If they can put a man on the moon, why can't they make a decent foot?" (Berger, 2014, p. 11).

Soon, he realized he would have to own this question and shift his thinking: "To do this, he had to make a change of pronouns: Specifically, he had to replace *they* with *I*"

(Berger, 2014, p. 14). For ten years, he kept asking questions, trying new prototypes, and falling again and again. His questions included:

> Why wood, when there are so many better alternatives? Why did a prosthetic foot have to be shaped like a human foot? Does that even make sense? Why was there so much emphasis on trying to match the look of a human foot? Wasn't performance more important? (Berger, 2014, p. 29)

Instead of asking himself, *Why?* he began to ask himself, *What if?*: "What if you could somehow replicate a diving board's propulsive effect in a prosthetic foot? What if a human leg could be more like a cheetah's?" (Berger, 2014, p. 35). He soon realized that he needed to find a power source that would inform a prosthetic shape that enabled the leg to run. These queries prompted *How?* questions, which inevitably led to a C-shaped blade-like model that curves into a much smoother, more comfortable prosthesis. After decades of asking questions, Van Phillips now runs on the beaches of California, an activity he loved before his accident.

Berger's (2014) model of questioning starts with promoting *Why?* questions, continues with *What if?* or wondering questions, and finds innovation as inquiry shifts to *how* questions. Building a culture of questioning provides the foundation for innovation and more targeted instruction. Questions lead to *What's next?*—a central aspect of instructional agility.

## The Main Idea

Questions provide information and focus. They help both students and teachers connect ideas and find new ones. Instructional agility at its best uncovers how students make sense of their learning (precision), and then leads to action as teachers respond to new information about how students are thinking and learning (flexibility). The student response may be new questions, potential solutions, and new insights. A student response requires teachers to create the classroom conditions—structures, skills, and safety—that provide the avenue for students to build on their thinking and respond. And teachers' actions during their instructional maneuvers (in response to their interpretations of student questions, comments, actions) push student learning and understanding forward and deeper based on what they uncover. This flexibility is critical: both the questions teachers pose and the questions students ask provide insight into students' thinking. This in turn leads to the ways that teachers guide students to connect and invest in their learning, to think more critically, to achieve mastery, and to gain confidence.

# Connections to Other Tenets

Questioning is a strategy that both students and teacher utilize within instructional agility. Teachers design questions to engage learners in conversation or in written responses. Teachers also design the classroom conditions in which students ask questions. When students produce questions, they may be aiming to clarify, wonder, explore, evaluate, or even connect. In any case, teachers are constantly interpreting student-generated questions and responses to understand how students are making meaning. These interpretations lead to instructional maneuvers that inevitably push students forward in their thinking and understanding. As such, questioning in instructional agility is grounded primarily in two tenets: assessment architecture and accurate interpretation.

Assessment architecture is, in short, beginning with the end in mind. Teachers, ideally working in collaboration, identify and analyze standards (develop learning progressions to map the path to proficiency) to achieve during the targeted unit. From these standards and learning progressions, teachers design questions to embed within instruction and assessment with the goal of gathering evidence of how students are progressing toward achievement of the standard. This design work, or architecture, happens prior to the start of the unit.

Once the design is in place, the unit is ready to go. Planning is key to accurate and reliable interpretations. Teachers enact the plan flexibly so instructional maneuvers are expected and not an additional burden on instructional time.

Predetermined, embedded questions provide opportunities for teachers to make instructional decisions in response to students. Student learning is unpredictable. What helps one student learn is not always the same for other students. Instructionally agile teachers are constantly observing, interpreting, and responding to what students are saying, doing, or producing. Solid assessment architecture creates a clear plan, and instructional agility requires flexibility for teachers to interpret evidence generated from questioning to ensure high levels of learning for all students.

# Questioning in Action

Students learn so much from asking questions and feeling comfortable to do so (Ruiz-Primo & Li, 2011). This was true for a group of students at a high school in the Midwest who, after failing the topic multiple times, were taking a team-taught algebra class. After conducting focus groups with students in this class, questioning emerged as key to their success. They articulated repeatedly that teachers allowed them to ask questions and did not make them feel "stupid" when they had to ask multiple times. Students revealed that asking questions was what made this class different than most others. In fact, their teachers encouraged them to ask questions about their under-standing and to wonder about the mathematics concepts. They said that when they asked a question, they didn't feel like they should already know the answer.

Often, teachers and sometimes other students respond to questions with exas-peration. So, students eventually just stop asking because they feel like they should already know or out of fear that teachers or other students will meet their inquiry with a tone that makes them feel stupid (K. Hartje, personal communication, April 15, 2015). Mei Schulte (2009), a senior taking an English learner college essay writ-ing class, writes about the feeling of not being able to ask questions: "She taught quickly and expected us to keep up. I remember needing help once, and when I had mustered up the courage to ask her, she explained it, but her tone said, 'Why don't you get this? I shouldn't have to explain this again'" (Schulte, 2009). Students are incredibly insightful into what helps them learn and engage and what gets in the way.

In fact, these student voices echo in the research of Maria Araceli Ruiz-Primo and Min Li (2011), who found that using questions to generate more dialogue prompted what she called *assessment conversations*. These conversations gave teachers (and stu-dents) insight into how to learn more. As a result, her findings, along with those of Arthur Applebee, Judith Langer, Martin Nystrand, and Adam Gamoran (2003), Nystrand and Gamoran (1991), and Ruiz-Primo and Erin Marie Furtak (2006, 2007), suggest that when students and teachers engage in more assessment conver-sations, achievement is higher (Heritage, 2013). Questions used to elicit evidence of learning and to generate dialogue provide a window (for teachers) and a mirror (for students) into student thinking, which sets teachers up to make instructional moves that inspire learning and meaning.

This learning and meaning foster engagement. Cassandra Scharber, Cynthia Lewis, Tracey Psycher, and Kris Isaacson (2016) explore the complex interactions among school, community, technology, questions, engagement, and their potential to situate students as knowledge producers, meaning makers, and creators through technology and issues of social justice. They tap into David J. Shernoff's (2013) definition of engagement as "the heightened, simultaneous experience of concentration, interest, and enjoyment in the task at hand" (p. 12, as cited in Scharber et al., 2016, pp. 195–196). They surmise that engagement is a critical characteristic of higher achievement and confidence:

> Engagement has been identified as one of the most significant predic-tors of learning and achievement among youth (Finn & Zimmer, 2012; Skinner & Pitzer, 2012). Kelly and Price (2014) found that engagement levels decline by almost 10% as youth transition to high school settings,

and according to Kelm and Connell (2004), once in high school, 40–60%
of students are chronically disengaged. (Scharber et al., 2016, p. 196)

Questions help shed light on students' proficiency levels, but they also help uncover what interests students and what they are curious about. When teachers see questions as a way to student engagement and achievement, they tap into their power—both as a way to understand learning to facilitate more learning, and as a way to hook students into thinking about interesting things and important issues that make the local and global world a better place. Scharber and colleagues (2016) find, as similar studies have, that when students are "provided opportunities to create and solve problems using technology" (p. 196), they are more likely to engage in learning. Questions sit at the foot of engagement and uncover student thinking to help them learn more and see themselves as contributors.

Questions, when teachers design and use them to promote instructional agility, are positioned to do three things: (1) provide evidence of learning, (2) foster engagement, and (3) promote dialogue. Each of these three components contributes to fostering hope and achievement for all students.

## Questions as Evidence of Learning

Both teacher-designed and student-generated questions can provide meaningful information that leads to deeper insight into how learning is happening and what might prompt greater learning: "A central practice in formative assessment is teachers' generation and collection of information about how learning is developing while instruction is underway" (Heritage, 2013, p. 179). Instructional agility in the form of questioning is a key attribute of getting quality information during the process of instruction.

For questions to act as evidence of learning, teachers intentionally plan questions, interpret responses, and communicate next steps. This is where the intersection with the other tenets comes into play. Assessment architecture, which teachers plan in advance (or co-construct with students), includes standards (bigger descriptions of learning) and learning targets (individual learning goals necessary to achieve the bigger ideas or standards).

As teachers work collaboratively to identify these standards, they think through what achievement or mastery looks like in student work: what they produce, what they say, and how they act. In essence, they are identifying what success looks like. As deeper clarity emerges of how students might learn key concepts, teachers get an idea of what questions to pose and what to listen for to uncover *how* students are understanding those concepts.

This leads to another tenet that is essential to instructional agility—accurate interpretation. When teachers pose questions or ask students to do so, they have to interpret students' responses in ways that lead to action that makes a difference. Teachers interpret, diagnose, connect, and then maneuver to help students make connections and learn more. Once teachers interpret the results, they can clearly *communicate* feedback, pose another question, or provide an example that helps students understand their strengths and next steps, no matter how far along students are in their learning. In summary, instructional agility depends on a clear assessment architecture (focused standards and evidence), accurate interpretation (teasing out what students know and what they need to do next), and clear communication about those interpretations (through feedback or self-assessment and self-regulation).

For example, look at one of the following Next Generation Science Standards (NGSS, 2013) for fourth graders.

> Make observations and/or measurements to provide evidence of the effects of weathering or the rate of erosion by water, ice, wind, or vegetation. (4-ESS2–2)
>
> Analyze and interpret data from maps to describe patterns of Earth's features. (4-ESS2–2)

In collaborative planning, the fourth-grade teacher team might identify the following learning targets that students must achieve to master these standards. This is called assessment architecture.

- I can use what I know about the earth's features and how they change to identify problems, make predictions, and pose solutions.

- I can interpret data from maps of the earth to describe changes over time.

- I can interpret data from maps to describe patterns and changes in the earth.

- I can use observations and evidence to draw conclusions about the effects of erosion and weathering on the earth.

- I can describe observations and how they connect to my question.

- I can identify quality observations from opinions or unrelated observations.

- I can describe weathering and how it affects the earth.

- I can describe erosion and how it is measured.

The teacher team ensures students master these learning targets throughout the fourth-grade science unit. These learning targets guide the questions they might predesign and pose to students (assessment architecture: design).

Figure 3.1 identifies the questions a teacher might pose during a fourth- grade geography lesson to elicit evidence of learning. The teacher ties the questions to the learning target and provides a purpose statement to show how this might happen during instruction. As the dialogue ensues, he or she probes and explains based on the overall purpose and identified learning target. This intentional design of assessment questions to pose during instruction helps teachers understand student learning.

| Learning Target | Questions | Purpose |
| --- | --- | --- |
| I can describe erosion and how it is measured. | What is erosion, and how is it measured? | Teachers pose this question to student pairs for dialogue. Teachers eavesdrop on the dialogue and then wrap up the discussion with a minilecture on erosion and how it is measured. |
| I can describe weathering and how it affects the earth. I can describe erosion and how it is measured. | What is the difference between weathering and erosion? | Teachers use this as an exit ticket to check for understanding on the concept of erosion. All students must understand this concept in order to interpret and make predictions. Teachers talk to individual students who do not master the concept. |
| I can interpret data from maps to describe patterns and changes in the earth. | Compare the interpretation statements you made with those of your partner's. How are they the same and different? | Teachers can use this activity to find out if students understand interpretation and can read a map. Through student dialogue and interpretation, teachers see who can identify what the maps actually say, who can make statements that show relationships (clear evidence they can interpret), and who can draw conclusions or think like a scientist. |
| I can use data interpreted from maps of the earth to describe changes over time. | How do interpretation statements help us understand how the earth has changed over time? | Students work in collaborative groups to discuss this question. To make predictions, teachers check whether students can see the changes and patterns that emerged over time. They may even generate a model to represent the changes. |

*Figure 3.1: Questions to elicit evidence of student learning.* continued ➔

| Learning Target | Questions | Purpose |
|---|---|---|
| I can use what I know about the earth's features and how they change to identify problems, make predictions, and pose solutions. | Why are erosion and weathering a threat to the earth? Back up your thinking with evidence from our readings and investigations. | In groups of three, students explore this question and identify evidence. The teacher collects the questions that arise and uses them to encourage further thinking as students engage in small-group dialogue. |
| I can use what I know about the earth's features and how they change to identify problems, make predictions, and pose solutions. | What questions might a scientist ask to try to predict the impact of erosion on the earth over the next two hundred years? | Teachers use these questions to determine the level of understanding students have about how the earth is changing. Teachers use surface-level questions to show students how to trace the data. They use deeper-level questions to generate dialogue in the classroom. |

*Source: Adapted from GLOBE Program, n.d.*

*Visit **go.SolutionTree.com/assessment** for a free reproducible version of this figure.*

Teachers generate questions to listen carefully to how students make meaning. Students generate questions for three purposes: (1) to clarify content or concepts, (2) to satisfy curiosity or interest, and (3) to problem-solve and connect. All purposes are insightful and can help teachers interpret how students engage, or do not engage, in learning. The second and third purposes lead to deep engagement and increased learning.

## Questions to Foster Engagement

The more teachers can get students engaged, the more students persist in their learning. This persistence helps them achieve more. Warren Berger (2014) writes:

> [Dan] Rothstein believes that questions do *something*—he is not sure precisely what—that has an "unlocking" effect in people's minds. "It's an experience we've all had at one point or another." Rothstein maintains, "Just asking or hearing a question phrased a certain way produces an almost palpable feeling of discovery and new understanding. Questions produce the light bulb effect." (pp. 16–17)

Scharber and colleagues (2016) describe a classroom culture that encourages questions and wondering, that leads to deep investment and engagement, and takes discussion and inquiry to a deeper level. Here's how it played out:

> One day while another group of learners led a presentation comparing private and public clean up assistance for Hurricane Katrina victims, Janessa

took out her smartphone and searched other charity foundation websites in an attempt to both complicate and reinforce the group's argument that charity foundations like the Red Cross spend too much money on administrative overhead compared to actual money reaching the hurricane's victims. This action by Janessa was not prompted by Ms. Vasich or other students but rather was mediated by the classroom activity (student presentation), technology access (smartphone), a motivating topic steeped in issues of social injustice (racialized victims of Hurricane Katrina), and a classroom culture of social critique (the act of finding other charity foundations' misuse of funds). . . . When Janessa dropped in a new, unsolicited intertextual connection about the Red Cross, she managed to turn the entire discussion toward a critique of the use of funds rather than a simpler and less critical discussion of differences between public and private responsibility for hurricane victims. . . . Importantly, neither the student presenters nor the teacher interrupted this move. In fact, the conversations turned toward Janessa's intertextual integration and other students quickly began to research other foundations and their uses of money via smartphones in real-time response to each other. We understood this moment to be an example of deeply authentic engagement. (Scharber et al., 2016, pp. 203–204)

The culture that the teacher had created in this classroom inspired a student to generate a question that turned the conversation to deep engagement. As teachers promote this type of questioning, they can be observing and probing to understand the extent to which students are achieving the essential learning the teachers intend.

## Questions to Promote Dialogue

When students start talking, teachers get a clearer sense of what they understand and how they are making sense of things. In quality formative assessment practice, teachers gain information about what students know and what they need to do next to grow and learn more. Questions are a central aspect of dialogue. To promote dialogue, students must learn how to ask questions that fulfill multiple purposes.

- Questions that probe for clarification make teachers more mindful of the extent to which students understand concepts.

- Questions that probe for debate push the dialogue to encourage multiple perspectives and can end in a lively discussion. This is useful when the debate is based in evidence and not just opinion or emotion.

- Questions that help develop innovative or new ideas pose *what if* scenarios that lead to productive collaboration and problem solving.

- Questions that dig into the causes and effects of various situations or phenomena help develop analysis and critical-thinking skills.

When students pose these types of questions, it helps teachers understand how they are or are not making meaning. Figure 3.2 offers question stems that teachers can use to develop a culture in which dialogue becomes a rich source of information and learning.

| Question Type | Question Stem |
|---|---|
| Clarifying Questions | What do you mean by . . . ?<br>What is an example of . . . ? |
| Debate Questions | What would another perspective look like . . . ?<br>What is the counter argument . . . ? |
| Innovation Questions | What if . . . ?<br>How might we . . . ? |
| Causal Questions | How does that connect to . . . ?<br>Why did that happen . . . ? |
| Analysis Questions | What would have changed if . . . didn't happen?<br>What were the contributing factors to . . . and how did that affect . . . ?<br>What is the relationship among these components . . . ? |

**Figure 3.2:** *Types of questions to promote dialogue.*

*Visit* **go.SolutionTree.com/assessment** *for a free reproducible version of this figure.*

# Strategies and Tools

For questions to be a valuable aspect of effective instructional agility, teachers must intentionally develop a questioning classroom culture. Skills, strategies, and safety must be front and center. In many cases, the majority of questions teachers ask have one right answer. On the other hand, open-ended questions have greater potential to reveal students' thinking patterns and how they are making sense of what they are learning. Teachers should identify the types of questions that are relevant to the specific discipline or inquiry, and then teach students what those questions are and what purpose they serve. They might even track the questions that students ask in the classroom. What kinds of questions do they ask? Who is asking them? Are the questions eliciting evidence of learning, engagement, and dialogue? If not, students may need direct instruction on quality questions, practice in asking and responding to them, and feedback to improve their questioning skills.

Teachers should develop routines and strategies for questioning. The strategies in the remaining pages of this chapter outline how to potentially structure instruction and assessment so students learn how to respond to and ask questions. Educators develop a richer questioning culture by creating a safe and inviting environment for questioning. When teachers seek to generate a learning-rich environment, their tone must not indicate exasperation or impatience with questioning. Teachers create different routines and procedures to foster questioning as a key to understanding how their students are learning and understanding.

Teachers can use the following strategies to gather information on how students understand a learning target that is essential to their achievement, leading to specific teacher and student responses. This information allows teachers to be more instructionally agile as they move through their instruction.

## Strategy 1: T-Chart

Consider this scenario: a fourth grader is struggling through reading a text about the earth's moon. After he finishes reading, he is supposed to answer questions that have a right or wrong answer. It becomes clear that he is only reading to answer the questions at the end of the passage. While his answers to the questions reveal something about his understanding, it is the thinking behind *why* he selects them that will inform instruction and provide a response that meets his needs.

Thus emerges a moment for the teacher to move to a T-chart. In the first column of the chart, the fourth-grade student writes what the text is saying—phrases or words tracking what he thinks is happening in the text. In the second column, he generates questions—both clarifying and *what if* questions or *I wonder* . . . statements. After each paragraph, the student stops and jots down a few notes in each column. Not only is he more deeply engaged in the text, but his questions become more complex and interesting.

As a whole class engages in an activity like this, the teacher monitors the charts to understand how each student comprehends the text through their statements and questions. The teacher could pose questions to the rest of the class to inspire dialogue or to become exit slips for all students. Those responses would offer the teacher a deeper understanding of how students engage with the text. Figure 3.3 (page 74) is an example of what this might look like for students.

This strategy helps students structure their thinking about the reading—to understand both how they comprehend the text (or any piece of information—it could be a data set from a science experiment, a cartoon, or other textual representations) and where they might find connections or new interests to explore. This information can prompt the teacher to clarify or push students into deeper thinking. The response happens *in the moment* as the teacher observes the kinds of questions students write or collect to analyze more closely the extent to which students understand the targeted concept.

| What is the text saying? | What questions emerge as you read? |
|---|---|
| Write words or phrases that remind you what the text says. | Ask questions or pose *I wonder . . .* statements as you read, listen, or watch. |
| | |

**Figure 3.3:** *T-chart reflection.*

*Visit* **go.SolutionTree.com/assessment** *for a free reproducible version of this figure.*

## Strategy 2: Reciprocal Questions

When students generate questions, they consider what they already know or have experienced with the targeted topic or learning. This leads to deeper learning and engagement. James Allen and Yan Dai (2016) studied both U.S. and Chinese college students' learning and engagement using a reciprocal questioning technique. The goal of reciprocal questioning is to use student-generated questions to promote collaborative discussions in academic disciplines through reading various texts.

For this strategy, the teacher asks students to generate questions about the chosen topic prior to reading. Students read texts about that topic and then meet in small groups in which they use their questions to engage in discussion. Meanwhile, the teacher monitors comprehension in the groups. Then the session closes with the teacher providing a minilecture on the key concepts and any follow-up to what he or she heard during small-group discussions. Following are some generic question stems teachers can use to develop higher-order thinking skills (King, 1990):

- How would you use . . . to . . .?
- What is a new example of . . .?
- Explain why . . . .
- What do you think would happen if . . .?
- What is the difference between . . . and . . .?
- How are . . . and . . . similar?
- What is a possible solution to the problem of . . .?
- What conclusions can you draw about . . .?
- How does . . . affect . . .?
- In your opinion, which is best: . . . or . . .? Why?
- What are the strengths and weaknesses of . . .?

- Do you agree or disagree with this statement?: . . . Support your answer.
- How is . . . related to . . . that we studied earlier? (p. 669)

Alison King's (2002) research on reciprocal questioning finds that students retain information longer and develop critical-thinking and problem-solving skills when questioning prior to and while reading texts versus questioning after reading texts. Allen and Dai (2016) report:

> The majority of learners both in the U.S. and in China found that the reciprocal questioning activity helped them learn academic content at a deeper level of understanding, helped them to envision how they might use what they learned in personal and professional ways, helped them monitor and regulate their learning, and increased their motivation to learn. (p. 1)

Figure 3.4 provides a chart teachers can use with students to focus the reciprocal-questioning assessment. While this is focused on text, mathematics content could also work with this strategy as students explore the concepts in context.

---

Name: _____ Date: _____

**Learning Targets:** (What do I want students to learn from reading this text?)

**Focus Text:**

**Directions:** Before you read the focus text, generate questions in the first column. Once you generate the questions, read the text. As you read, write notes about your questions and additional questions to pose to small groups of students. During class, pose questions to students and elicit conversation. Add ideas and insights to your chart. Finally, provide a minilecture based on what you hear during the discussion. In the rightmost column, students write notes and new insights as the teacher lectures on the questions they generated.

| Questions Prior to Reading the Text | Ideas From Questions During Small-Group Discussion; Additional Questions | Notes During the Follow-Up Minilecture |
|---|---|---|
| | | |
| | | |
| | | |
| | | |

---

***Figure 3.4:*** *Reciprocal-questioning chart.*

*Visit **go.SolutionTree.com/assessment** for a free reproducible version of this figure.*

## Strategy 3: Hinge Questions

Unlike reciprocal questions, hinge questions help teachers conduct a quick and effective check on student understanding. These are teacher-generated questions. A synonym for *hinge* is *pivot*, a word that illustrates the purpose of a hinge question. It provides a moment for teachers to gather information from students on a critical concept and enables them to pivot in their instructional moves to respond to student learning (or misconceptions). These questions give teachers insight into each learner—not just the class in general—regarding a key concept. Sometimes, these hinge questions generate dialogue among students so teachers can eavesdrop and get a sense of misconceptions and understanding and then interpret student learning and respond to help students grow. These questions act as a quick check on understanding and to generate dialogue and provide feedback about where students are in their learning. Teachers can consider the following three key ideas when developing hinge questions.

1. In planning a lesson, identify the learning targets (assessment architecture). Decide which learning targets are essential or which concepts are so important that you need to stop and check for understanding during the lesson.

2. Design a hinge question that will effectively reveal each student's level of understanding. Pose a question and then craft *distractors* (incorrect responses) that reveal something about a student's understanding or misconceptions. Wiliam (2015) eloquently states:

   We have to take great care in designing hinge questions so learners don't get the correct answer for the wrong reason. This is perhaps the most important property of a good question. After all, if learners with the right thinking and those with the wrong thinking can answer a question in the same way, it's not very valuable as a diagnostic tool. The aim is always to have learners with the right thinking and learners with the wrong thinking give different answers. (p. 42)

   The examples in figure 3.5 show statements, misconceptions (plausible distractors), and some accompanying interpretations that can help teachers determine how to pivot and help students grow.

   Consider crafting questions that have more than one right answer. This can generate dialogue and debate among students, which further sheds light on the level of understanding they have. Teachers listen in with intentional focus on the kinds of comments they can interpret and respond to in order to push learning.

3. Based on student responses to the questions, you can decide to go forward or go back (Wiliam, 2015). This principle is the core of designing and using hinge questions.

| | Which of the following pairs of fractions are equivalent? | |
|---|---|---|
| | **Statement** | **Misconception—Plausible Distractor** |
| A. | $^3/_7$ $^7/_3$ | Reciprocal fractions are equivalent. |
| B. | $^6/_8$ $^{12}/_{16}$ | **This is the correct answer.** |
| C. | $^4/_9$ $^7/_9$ | Common denominators mean equivalency. |
| D. | $^{10}/_{12}$ $^{10}/_{17}$ | Common numerators mean equivalency. |

| | Which of the following best supports the purpose of starting the Soccer Without Borders program? (Students reference the text they just read.) | |
|---|---|---|
| | **Statement** | **Misconception—Plausible Distractor** |
| A. | Coach Ben sets out guidelines that the players must follow: healthy eating, a helping spirit, and above all, a respectful treatment of others on and off the field. | This is a strategy used in the program. |
| B. | Omar Benitez is one student who has benefited from the program. The eighteen-year-old from Colombia made his first school friend (from Liberia) on the soccer team. | This is an example or supporting detail of the main idea but not the purpose. This student needs to work on understanding the difference between specific details and a general purpose. |
| C. | Coach Ben helped Benitez prepare for his SAT exams and apply for college scholarships. Benitez said that Coach Ben has become like a second father to him. | This is a detail that further describes the outcome of the program but again, it's a specific detail but not the purpose. |
| D. | Now the players are working together off the field. They want to convince the school district to give them a field to play on. | This describes the program's purpose. **It is the best answer.** |

| | **Statement** | **Misconception—Plausible Distractor** |
|---|---|---|
| A. | | |
| B. | | |
| C. | | |
| D. | | |

*Source: Adapted from Vagle, 2015.*

**Figure 3.5: Hinge question template.**

*Visit **go.SolutionTree.com/assessment** for a free reproducible version of this figure.*

### Strategy 4: Ask Me a Question

Dave Sladkey is a high school mathematics teacher in Naperville, Illinois, who writes the popular blog *Reflections of a High School Math Teacher*. He wrote a 2016 post in which he responds to a tweet that suggested teachers ask two hundred questions per day, and students ask, on average, two questions per week. Knowing the power of questioning for learning and engagement—for teachers and especially students—he shared the statistics with his daughter. She responded by asking, "Why don't you *require* students to ask questions?"

Building on his daughter's question and a suggestion from his colleague, Rachel Fruin, to use the strategy *Ask me a question*, Sladkey found a way to prompt richer discussions in his mathematics class. By requiring students to ask questions, he reported gaining a whole new insight into some of his quietest students. Equally important, he discovered the need to teach students how to ask higher-level questions, and he observed the power of questions to reveal a student's understanding.

At first, teachers may find it necessary to use one of the question prompts we provided earlier in this chapter, since it may take students some time to get used to this new instructional routine. If students didn't have questions, Sladkey had them talk in pairs first to explore possible questions. If he didn't have them talk in pairs first, he learned to return to students who didn't have an initial question to ask again after a few others posed their questions. Dialogue increased in the class, and it was a new way to uncover students' depth of learning (Sladkey, 2016). This strategy is about creating structures to help students generate questions as they are learning.

## Conclusion

A culture of questioning—in which there is more than one right answer and space to consider and "sit with" the questions—is not easy in a world where the answers to so many questions are readily available. In many cases, the answers or potential solutions are more about asking more questions and discerning credible sources and meaningful information than whether the answer is right or wrong. Whether teacher or student generated, questions provide rich sources of information about student learning. When teachers interpret and analyze them to understand how students are progressing in their understanding of the targeted learning, questions provide rich sources of information to guide instruction and help teachers respond to students' evolving understanding as they experience classrooms and instruction.

# Pause and Ponder

Take a few moments to reflect on the following questions.

- Describe the key characteristics of effective questioning practice that promotes instructional agility.

- Which questioning purpose (eliciting evidence, fostering engagement, or generating dialogue) is most common in your classroom? Which are you underutilizing?

- What kinds of questions are students asking? What kinds of questions are you asking? Use our categories to track the frequency and type of questions you and your students are asking.

- What current questioning procedures and protocols exist in your classroom or school? What might be important to develop?

- How could you use questions in your course or grade level to develop more innovative ideas? How could you use them to understand how students are learning?

# CHAPTER 4
# OBSERVING

*You can observe a lot by watching.*

—Yogi Berra

Observing is what coaches do, whether it's in real time or through video recordings. Certainly, long-term planning and long-term improvements come about when coaches consistently examine video of past games because it allows them to watch their athletes perform the same moment multiple times at various speeds. However, the art of coaching actually lies in the *moments* when coaches identify a discrepancy between the desirable performance and what the athlete just did and use that information to promote continued improvement. Athletes perform and rarely produce any kind of tangible evidence of their skills; a tennis coach doesn't ask his or her athletes to write a paragraph about their serving ability, for example. While coaches employ a variety of tools to help focus their attention on what truly matters, the *art* of coaching is in the real-time maneuvers coaches make in service of their individual athletes and teams.

Coaches epitomize instructional agility because their focus is on immediate improvement without the need to necessarily document every move an athlete makes. Obviously, there are a lot of useful data available to coaches, especially at the collegiate and professional levels, but the data aren't always granular enough for moment-to-moment improvements. Developing this kind of *read-and-react* coaching mindset can introduce a powerful aspect of formative assessment often missing from even the most effective teachers' repertoires.

For teachers, thoughts of assessment typically drift toward students producing something tangible. Whether it be a traditional test, project, research paper, or lab report, educators continue viewing assessment as a noun, and teachers expect that students will demonstrate their learning via a *thing* they turn in to the teacher.

Tangible evidence is advantageous for teachers because students can produce the evidence and teachers can assess the work independently. That said, tangible evidence is not the only sort of evidence that students can produce. Both informal and nonverbal evidence can also lead to instructional maneuvers that maximize the effectiveness and efficiency of the instructional process. Teachers, artists, musicians, woodworkers, machinists, and, of course, coaches use observation as an essential aspect of their instruction and craft. When one notices quality or misunderstanding and poses a question or makes a move to guide students to understand their next steps or correct their conceptual thinking, this is instructional agility. While this evidence is somewhat atypical when one compares it to the traditional teaching-learning-assessment processes, informal and nonverbal evidence is an essential part of being instructionally agile.

# The Main Idea

A collective move toward deeper learning means that teachers must require students to produce more complex demonstrations of learning related to both curricular content as well as with crosscurricular competencies (for example, critical thinking, innovation, and collaboration). As such, they must lean in favor of more performance assessments that go beyond both the simplicity of selected response and the often singularly focused constructed response–type questions (for example, a paragraph to answer one specific content question). Teachers often anchor performance assessments around demonstrations they can touch, see, or hear in order to assess them. While the tangible demonstration is fairly traditional and familiar to most teachers, the focus for this chapter is on the latter two: demonstrations of learning the teacher observes (that is, sees or hears) in order to assess. This observation provides prime opportunities for instructional agility, particularly informal and nonverbal observation.

## Informal Observation

Whether students speak in a foreign language or serve a volleyball, teachers of those subjects are often well versed in planning and executing formal assessments for subject-specific skills. The area most often in need of strengthening is the more informal type of assessment in which real-time observations lead to an immediate instructional maneuver. Informal is not the same as random or haphazard; the teacher still observes with purpose. Teachers respond throughout their instruction with intentionality by observing what students say and do to determine how learners are receiving and processing information.

## Nonverbal Observation

When master teachers observe learners, they pay as much attention to what is said as to what is not said. Nonverbal cues often reveal how learners are processing information. This is when a teacher's relationship with students pays dividends, as student dispositions, motivations, and other idiosyncratic responses can impact instructional maneuvers. Even within strong student-teacher relationships, students are not always honest about their levels of understanding or their levels of hope and efficacy. It is not uncommon for students to remain externally stoic while experiencing internal turmoil.

The stronger the relationship, the more likely it is that teachers will pick up on the nonverbal cues (such as facial expressions) that tell the truth and stand in contrast to what students are saying. Sometimes being instructionally agile has less to do with evidence of learning and more to do with evidence of the *student*. Observing the student with awareness of this dynamic helps teachers really focus on student disposition and affect and remain poised to respond at a moment's notice.

# Connections to Other Tenets

The most important assessment tenets for the instructionally agile and observational teacher include *assessment architecture, accurate interpretation*, and *communication*. The level of intentionality required for assessment via observation requires that teachers pay close attention to crafting an assessment plan that builds *observable* moments into the instructional sequence. For students, demonstrations of learning may feel informal and even random, but teachers feel the sense of formality because they have left nothing to chance.

Effective and efficient assessment is always planned and purposeful, so despite the untraditional feel of these assessment moments, teachers must still execute with that purpose in mind. As relationships strengthen, teachers can more intentionally choose when, how, and even whom to observe for those nonverbal responses that provide meaningful insight to students' learning.

Interpreting assessment results is also paramount and definitely linked to architecture. When they design assessments on the front end, teachers must establish clear criteria so the interpretation—either direct or inferred—is on point for the subsequent instructional maneuvers. Without clear criteria, teachers can miss critical moments during informal assessment and misinterpret critical emotional reactions. So much of interpreting informal and nonverbal assessment moments begins with correctly interpreting observations. Incorrect interpretations of informal assessment can lead to incorrect instructional maneuvers; incorrect interpretations of nonverbal cues can weaken the relationship between teachers and students.

Finally, communicating results is important with observation because so many maneuvers will be in real time, which means timing is everything. Observing non-verbal reactions is also important, especially those indicating students' level of frustration with the lack of or limited progress they are making. Given the obvious sensitivity of those moments, teachers must navigate their communication of what they observed with finesse, especially if those moments are summative and meant to verify that learning has occurred. Teachers who plan, interpret, and communicate with both intentionality and sensitivity can take advantage of the informal and non-verbal moments crucial to student success.

# Observing in Action

Since observation happens naturally, teachers seldom cultivate its practice as a formal assessment strategy, especially during informal or nonperformance-based moments. As a result, potentially powerful learning opportunities can be lost. Teachers gain the ability to be more instructionally agile when they intentionally observe learning indicators in formal and informal moments. Margaret Heritage (2013) reinforces this point when she states, "Teachers engage in continually taking stock of learning by paying close, firsthand attention to specific aspects of students' developing understanding and skills as teaching and learning is [sic] taking place in real time" (p. 179).

In formal assessment situations, teachers use observation to identify a student's current level of proficiency. In informal situations, teachers generally use observation to seek evidence of a student's level of understanding, or note points of confusion or common misunderstandings as they emerge. Teachers also use emerging evidence to determine the effectiveness of their instruction.

Unlike casual viewing, observing involves seeking evidence for a specific purpose in a particular way. The way teachers determine the *exact purpose in a particular way* varies based on whether the emerging evidence is predetermined (planned, formal assessment experiences) or naturally evolving (informal, unplanned, but informative moments). In a formal assessment experience, for example, a teacher determines the conditions and criteria for the performance and then monitors students' performances for the identified variables. At the conclusion of a formal assessment observation, teachers then provide feedback, marks, grades, or scores based on the predetermined criteria and conditions.

In an informal learning moment, however, teachers seldom plan for unsolicited emerging evidence (for example, feedback, questions, and quizzical looks) and must be prepared to acknowledge, interpret, and respond to it in immediate and appropriate ways. In such teaching moments, teachers' generalizable purpose is always to gauge understanding or identify feelings. They use observation to explore comments or questions students share with peers or with them. Likewise, they continually gauge nonverbal cues to more deeply investigate what students *aren't* saying. Whether teachers manage it in formal or informal moments, observation is a powerful formative assessment strategy that no teachers should leave to happenstance.

In most cases, formality, or practice, refers to teachers intentionally planning and organizing students' development of specific skills. Sometimes this means developing skills within specific targets or standards. In other cases, such as with games, the teachers plan the overall experience, but the minutiae are unpredictable; this is when teachers must be ready to make real-time adjustments. In either case, the teacher has a clear idea of what the ideal performance *should* look like (criteria) and reacts to what he or she observes (instructional agility) to determine the next step toward success. Most often, teachers react instantly, orally describing what to do next along a positive growth trajectory. While the context may be different, the process of observation and agile response in more formal performance settings is identical.

Formal performance observations require teachers to make a number of decisions surrounding the kinds of inferences necessary to ensure accurate assessment (Lane, 2010). What separates performance assessments from most other assessment methods is the sophisticated number of inferences teachers require. Certainly, other assessment methods, namely selected and constructed responses, also require a level of inference, but not at the same level of depth or breadth required during a formal performance in which the teacher *is* the link between the performance and the success criteria.

This is where validity issues can arise as a result of inaccurate inferences that may happen when teachers misinterpret the criteria (Cizek, 2009; Kane, 2006) or include irrelevant features not reflected in the original success criteria (Messick, 1994). These irrelevant features could include, but are not limited to, desirable aesthetics or behavioral dispositions. They can cause the best-laid assessment plans to unravel. Research continues to indicate that the collective level of teacher assessment competency, especially when requiring inferences, still needs strengthening (Campbell, 2013; Campbell & Evans, 2000; Cizek, 2000).

Several elements are needed for teachers to make effective observations: intent, clarity, and nonverbal cues.

# Intent

Addressing accuracy issues begins when teachers understand the specific *intent* of the performance. If the intent is an overall generalization, then the performance requires an adequate sampling across the domain (Lane, 2013). For example, students would need to serve a volleyball, speak in a foreign language, or even cut wood enough times for the teacher to accurately gauge the performance level; a single instance would be insufficient. This is essential when the intended purpose of the performance is summative; an overall judgment needs to fully encapsulate the standards' scope.

Intended finite performances (not generalizing) can also be a part of the summative process. However, the primary purpose of finite performances would be formative because they don't often include the full scope of the standards. Whether teachers are assessing students in nonverbal communication during a presentation, the position of their elbows while shooting a basketball, or their ability to drill symmetrical holes to assemble a shelf, the intent is for the teacher to assess at a more granular level to ascertain students' acquisition of specific skills that underpin the full extent of the standard.

# Clarity

Once teachers determine *intent*, they must attend to clarity in terms of what they are assessing through observation. Robert Mislevy, Linda Steinberg, and Russell Almond (2003) submit that teachers must be purposeful about designing performance assessments in which they have clearly identified cognitive demands, which means articulating the content and cognitive processes that they will assess are essential.

Once teachers identify content and cognitive processes, they then describe the performances that allow them to assess the content and processes, as well as what task would elicit such performances. In other words, teachers must link the tasks to a specific set of performance criteria that allow them to assess both content and cognitive processes. Critical to this process is identifying performance criteria because it is through these clear criteria that teachers accurately assess their students.

Assessment through observation is about inferring quality performances. When developing clear criteria, teachers can essentially follow a three-step process for establishing a construct-centered approach, as Samuel Messick (1994) describes:

> A construct-centered approach [to assessment design] would begin by asking what complex of knowledge, skills, or other attributes should be assessed, presumably because they are tied to explicit or implicit objectives of instruction or are otherwise valued by society. Next, what behaviors or performances should reveal those constructs, and what tasks or situations should elicit those behaviors? Thus, the nature of the construct guides the selection or construction of relevant tasks as well as the rational development of construct-based scoring criteria and rubrics. (p. 16)

Each layer operates a more finite level of specificity. The tasks elicit the performances, which then allow teachers to assess students' knowledge, skills, and other attributes more accurately. Teachers establish criteria—which they often communicate in rubric form—at the performance level, rather than the task level; this allows them to apply criteria longitudinally across multiple tasks, and prevents them having to repeatedly teach the criteria with every new task. As students continually engage in these performances with similar criteria, they receive nuanced feedback that teachers provide as they observe. Students achieve at higher levels as they get opportunities to continually practice the same skill in multiple settings.

## Nonverbal Cues

There's always more to a message than the words expressed. Facial expressions, gestures, and the pitch, rate, or tone of a person's voice can change the positive message, "Great job!" into a snarly or sarcastic barb. In his research on effective communication, author Albert Mehrabian (1981) finds that when people communicate messages in the realm of feelings or attitudes, especially in a situation where words do *not* match the meaning, the nonverbal messages overpower the verbal. Specifically, nonverbal cues make up the majority of any message that involves feelings or attitudes.

- People generally glean 55 percent of a message from a person's facial expressions.

- People determine 38 percent of a message from paralinguistic patterns (the pitch, rate, and tone, or the *way* a person expresses the words).

- People determine only 7 percent of a message from the actual spoken words.

In other words, *what* a student says when thinking aloud, answering a teacher's questions, or expressing frustration with a concept is only a small component of the information a teacher must analyze when trying to make follow-up instructional maneuvers.

According to John Hattie and Gregory Yates (2014), teachers must build relationships with students as much to understand their interests and needs as to be able to interpret their nonverbal cues accurately. They note:

> Expert teachers are vigilant when it comes to monitoring learner learning and attention. . . . They keenly read individual facial expressions and are well aware that superficial aspects such as head nodding often mask genuine learning. They make constant instructional judgments to avoid overloading their learners, become highly adept at matching curriculum tasks to individual capabilities and in providing acknowledgment and feedback. They therefore are much more adept at knowing where each learner should go next—this proficiency to know "where to next" based on learners' actual achievement is a hallmark of their expertise. (p. 105)

It's important, then, for teachers to observe nonverbal cues as part of their instructional routine. The depth at which a teacher understands the learning needs and behaviors of each student can define the difference between proficient teaching and masterful teaching.

# Strategies and Tools

Learning to teach can be so challenging that often novice teachers begin by observing the students' visible behaviors—those that are immediately accessible and evident. Master teachers have learned to dig deeper and observe thinking. As they do, they are careful to examine the spoken and unspoken messages learners send while learning. Several strategies support teacher efforts in making thinking transparent.

## Strategy 1: Provide Targeted Feedback During Instruction

Observation provides teachers with an effective and efficient way to gather feedback and inform their maneuvers during instruction. It gives insight into students' thinking, which uncovers teachable moments. It requires a teacher to interpret students' actions and words in ways that lead to growth. Imagine a kindergarten classroom, for example, where students focus on gathering *juicy* words about color with the overall goal of using more descriptive words in their narrative writing. Students work at various stations around the room, and the teacher watches and interacts with them. One learner wanders throughout the room, clipboard in hand, searching for words to write. The teacher asks him a few questions, and he doesn't respond. Then she suggests a word from the color wall. After a few minutes, he pauses and asks, "What do you think would happen if you mixed blue with green?" He doesn't want just any word; instead, he wants to create his own word. At first glance, this boy looks like he is not following directions and is confused, perhaps not recognizing any words.

In many classrooms, this is the moment when teachers redirect or help students to follow the directions or complete the task. With just a few more minutes of observation, the student's deep analytic and thoughtful interpretation of the task produces something quite interesting. He meets the learning target, and the structure doesn't get in the way because there is space for him to create and interpret.

In the rush of completing tasks and assignments, teachers can create a culture in which students always need to get the right answer (there is a time and a place for the right answer—just not always) instead of thinking more deeply or allowing a little space to see what emerges. These observations provide insight into student learning—what they understand and what they still need to work on. Offering tasks and then creating space to watch and observe is another form of assessment that teachers can use formatively—they can use these descriptions of learning to understand where students are and where they need to go next.

Consider what could happen to this student if he continued to wander and have thoughts like this that teachers misinterpret as off task, misconceptions, or even defiance. Any one of these misinterpretations gives him signals about the value of his thoughts and his work. Too quickly, he may stop thinking deeply and either enter compliance mode and shift to finding the right answer or just stop trying because he doesn't find relevance or meaning. When teachers take time to observe and see possibilities (and transparently communicate this feedback), they give students hope and important information that help them thrive.

In order to target feedback from observations during the lesson, a teacher focuses on essential learning targets because they drive the kind of feedback and observations he or she chooses. Throughout lesson planning, how do teachers identify essential learning targets (assessment architecture) and build in activities that allow them to observe and respond to students about those targets? One strategy might be a calendar, as figure 4.1 shows, to map the days. The teacher would identify the learning target he or she would address each day, as well as the instructional activity. This provides focused direction for teacher attention.

| Monday | Tuesday | Wednesday | Thursday | Friday |
|---|---|---|---|---|
| October 4 | October 5 | October 6 | October 7 | October 8 |
| Learning target: I can show how the theme or central idea develops throughout the entire text. | Learning target: I can show how the theme or central idea develops throughout the entire text. | Learning target: I can show how the theme or central idea develops throughout the entire text. | Learning target: I can write an objective summary of the text. | Learning target: I can write an objective summary of the text. |
| Instructional activity: Partners read *The Gift of the Magi* and use graphic organizers to map the story. | Instructional activity: Students share graphic organizer maps and dialogue to compare and contrast their thinking. Following the dialogue, students revise their graphic organizers. | Instructional activity: Partners read an additional informational text that relates to the story's theme. | Instructional activity: Each student writes a summary of the text in a graphic organizer. The teacher observes summaries as students write to determine a minilesson for the next day. | Instructional activity: The teacher offers a minilesson based on what he or she saw in the summaries. Students then revise their summaries and develop questions or *I wonder* statements. |

*Figure 4.1: Calendar.*

continued ➜

| Monday | Tuesday | Wednesday | Thursday | Friday |
|---|---|---|---|---|
| October 11 | October 12 | October 13 | October 14 | October 15 |
| Learning target: I can analyze an author's meaning using explicit references from the text without summarization. | Learning target: I can analyze an author's meaning using explicit references from the text without summarization. | Learning target: I can analyze an author's meaning using explicit references from the text without summarization. | Learning target: I can draw inferences about the author's meaning and correctly cite several pieces of textual evidence to support my inferences. | Learning target: I can draw inferences about the author's meaning and correctly cite several pieces of textual evidence to support my inferences. |
| Instructional activity: Students use note cards to find and cite explicit references from the text that led to their summaries. | Instructional activity: The teacher takes explicit references from students and uses them to help small groups discuss the theme and text development. Each small group develops an image and a question to pose to another group. Each group gets a question from another, discusses it, and writes a response. | Instructional activity: Students read an informational text on the same theme. Students find text evidence that supports or counters the theme identified in *The Gift of the Magi*. | Instructional activity: Students write an inference or two from the note cards with textual evidence. In dialogue or writing, students explain someone else's potential inference. | Instructional activity: Teachers administer a summative assessment (over the next three days). Students choose another short story from a list. Students independently create a graphic organizer map with an objective summary. Students record a theme and how evidence from the text supports that theme. |

*Source: Vagle, 2014.*

*Visit **go.SolutionTree.com/assessment** for a free reproducible version of this figure.*

Observations such as this are rich ground for feedback. Hattie (2009) and Hattie and Timperley (2007) describe the power of feedback not only as information students receive so they can act but also as information teachers can use to inform their lesson planning and instructional responses.

Teachers often ask, "How do I provide feedback effectively and efficiently?" Teachers can generate feedback from observation rather than writing comments on every student's assessments outside of class. For example, a teacher might engage students in some type of collaborative or individual activity (focused on a learning target), and then prepare a chart of student names. As students proceed with the activity, the teacher notes individual understandings and misconceptions on the chart. Given these observations, the next day's lesson focuses on the insights he or she gathers. Not only does this help teachers focus lesson planning, it also reduces the amount of time they spend providing feedback on work they collect (and often take home).

Douglas Fisher and Nancy Frey (2012) offer another way to think through this notion of observation—it saves time and targets instruction. When considering a lesson and learning target, teachers identify common misconceptions and note which students they observe making these errors. This chart helps plan the next day's lesson—either more formally (with students working in groups) or individually (based on students' misconceptions). It could also serve as a reminder for the teacher to connect with individual students the following day. See the example in figure 4.2 from a science classroom. The chart shows students' initials by hour.

**Learning target:** I can describe and support the central argument of a scientific text.
Students read a text on the DNA findings that helped cancer research. They engage in small-group dialogue and then individually create a concept map with explanations. The teacher notes evidence of errors that students make by marking their initials on the chart.

| Error | Hour 1 | Hour 2 | Hour 3 | Hour 4 | Hour 5 |
|---|---|---|---|---|---|
| Summarizing the sequence of events | NT, SW | JS, LM | RR, TZ, SO, SJ, PW | JF, DS, MN, PS, LD, DD, FS, DA | |
| Identifying the general topic versus the argument | TN, KL, OH, AM, PS, GJ | GH | JK, LS, DD, BA, WD, FW, PS, NF | KL, DZ | FD, SK, BB, LD, ES, JO, PW, DS, KS |
| Providing general explanations that loosely connect with but don't support the argument | KS, TM, BH, WA, FD, TP, EW | PT, NV, LS, MW, FA | LS, RV | EF, PK, SW, GJ | NT, HJ, KW, VS, TU |
| Confidence: Students show mastery but are seeking approval or wanting someone else to tell them what to do. | | PT, NV | | SW, GJ | JC, NT, LE, RV, BD |

**Figure 4.2: Science lesson example.**                continued →

| Error | Hour 1 | Hour 2 | Hour 3 | Hour 4 | Hour 5 |
|---|---|---|---|---|---|
| Showing mastery | VC, MS, MW, ZP, EF, AD | PE, RV, CV, MV, LJ, DE | CC, BA, DD, WP, SS, VM | KL, MN, SD, ED, PS, OS | KL, DS |

*Source: Adapted from Fisher & Frey, 2012.*

## Strategy 2: Note Student Comments and Questions to Target Instruction

Observing or noticing student comments and questions can also provide feedback to the teacher. In this simulated example, a teacher charted over the course of a week what she noticed about the students' fluency, word use, comprehension, and connections. Such documentation will easily inform the literacy circles for the following week. See figure 4.3.

| Student Name | I can read words smoothly and with emotion. | I can explain the meaning of words I read in a text. | I can identify the main idea and details in a text or the characters and theme in a story. | I can make connections to what I read to other texts, characters, ideas, or experiences. |
|---|---|---|---|---|
| **Student A** | X | *predict, cherish* | X | *Connected to a book we read—Little Red Riding Hood* |
| **Student B** | X | *not cherish* | *Needs to work on important details from unimportant details* | *Reminded her of her grandmother* |
| **Student C** | X | *with prompting* | X | *Lots of prompting to connect* |
| **Student D** | X | *predict, fascinate* | *Work on theme* | *Insightful connection with character and a TV show* |

*Figure 4.3: Observing or noticing student comments and questions.*

These observations can help teachers group students by similar learning needs. They can also help teacher teams co-design instruction or interventions based on student learning needs. For example, after a few days of observation, a teacher may identify all the students who need to work on reading words smoothly and with emotion together. The teacher plans an instructional activity to help them work on this and then checks to see if they have improved after. Another group of students the teachers identified might need to distinguish between the main idea and important and unimportant details. This group of students would engage in an instructional activity that helps them work on this concept. Again, the teacher would check to see if the activity helped them grow in this concept. The teacher would form other groups as needed to address each student's learning needs. This type of observation leads to instructional agility in a targeted manner.

## Strategy 3: Use Digital Portfolios

Advancements in technology allow great ease of access for teachers, students, and parents. Now more than ever, creating an online, real-time, observable portfolio is possible and even desirable. Many of the available applications allow students and teachers to upload tangible artifacts, photos, drawings, and even videos. Some programs (for example, Seesaw; https://web.seesaw.me) even allow students to add their own voice-over commentary, text, or annotations to the uploaded items. These options allow students to describe what they are demonstrating so it appears seamless for teachers and parents.

It is prudent, however, to be mindful of the formative-summative relationship. Many digital portfolios can take on the *feel* of summative assessment because parents are often end users of the digital portfolios. If the portfolio includes formative demonstrations of learning, teachers must inform parents that these are *mid-learning* demonstrations and that they need not overreact to partial progress. Without guidance, it would be easy for parents and students to slip into feeling that students aren't learning fast enough. At their best, digital portfolios can be a window into the classroom that provides parents with an opportunity to see how their children are progressing and a mirror that helps students track their own learning.

## Strategy 4: Conference With a Note-Taking Tool

Conferences and conversations with students provide meaningful information about learning, confidence, and motivation. Teachers can build student conferences into the rhythm of classroom instruction during pivotal moments to promote student understanding.

For example, Margaret Heritage (2013) describes Ms. Alonzo's fifth-grade writing workshop. Ms. Alonzo identifies five students she wants to meet with during each writing workshop segment. She has a three-ring binder where she documents her observations and conversations.

Throughout each conference, she targets three things: (1) a compliment that specifically identifies and explains a strength, (2) a teaching moment (targeted explanation or concept the student needs), and (3) a description of what's next (that is, what she left the student to work on). We outline how a teacher might use this kind of framework for a student named Edgar in figure 4.4.

| Date | Compliment | Teaching Moment | What's Next? |
|------|-----------|-----------------|--------------|
| 1/12 | "Recognized the reliability of his source" (Heritage, 2013, p. 180) | "Discussed how evidence supported his argument" (Heritage, 2013, p. 180) | "Organization and transitional sentences" (Heritage, 2013, p. 180) |
| 1/24 | | | |
| | | | |
| | | | |

*Source: Heritage, 2013.*

**Figure 4.4: *Edgar's student conference learning document.***

Students could also keep this tool in a notebook, electronic portfolio, or three-ring binder to track their learning progress. Teachers could find this invaluable as they make observations and provide students with feedback in the moment (as well as during more scheduled conference times), and students could track their feedback and reflection.

## Strategy 5: Observe Nonverbal Cues

Teachers often employ anecdotal records to isolate key behaviors, gather data or identify patterns for informed decision making, and explore patterns for individuals or groups of students to better understand their learning tendencies. *Anecdotal records* are observational notes that the teacher writes or video, audio, or photos of students' words, behaviors, knowledge, or skills intended to document and support student learning. These records support teacher reflection regarding follow-up instructional maneuvers. They document and describe observable behaviors and patterns over time for a student or a group of students engaged in the learning process. The teacher usually records anecdotal notes during or after observing a learning experience.

The benefits of anecdotal records include the following.

- Identify instructional understandings and misunderstandings.
- Capture observations of significant behaviors that might otherwise be lost.
- Record information about student development over a period of time.
- Provide ongoing records of instructional needs.

Teachers can record anecdotal information by doing the following.

- Recording observations and the circumstances in which they occurred, noting the time, date, students' names, and so on

- Randomizing names or selecting key names for specific purposes and following through with documentation over a specific period of time

- Recording data in ways that are easily trackable and manipulated (for example, note cards, journal entries, digital spreadsheets, digital portfolios, or Google Forms)

- When possible, using consistent, structured forms to identify patterns over time

The templates in figures 4.5 (page 96), 4.6 (page 96), and 4.7 (page 97) show examples of how a teacher might collect anecdotal notes. Those notes might stem from *tells*—behaviors that reveal what someone is *not* saying.

Documenting anecdotal observations can provide powerful formative data to help teachers understand their students so, eventually, without relying on such templates, teachers can quickly gather and interpret emerging evidence about individual students *during* the learning process.

Figure 4.5 provides a way for teachers to familiarize themselves with a learner's nonverbal responses, or *tells*, when they are in the midst of learning. Tells (behaviors that reveal what someone is *not* saying) can demonstrate a student's experiences as he or she processes information. For example, a teacher might record what it looks like when a particular student is engaged in active learning—one student might doodle to support deep thinking, while another might cover his or her ears to drown out distractions.

Teachers can use figure 4.6 to gather frequency evidence about a problem or desired behaviors. For example, a teacher might track in a ten-minute period the number of times a student interrupts others in a conversation and use the evidence to help the student focus on changing this behavior. Likewise, a teacher might track the number of times a student is on task in a ten-minute period. Teachers can use this evidence to document behaviors relative to their given expectations so they can make informed decisions on how to move forward with instruction and learning.

Figure 4.7 is a variation of figure 4.6. It also helps teachers document behaviors relative to expectations, but they use it to improve program-level concerns (for example, is the curriculum engaging? Is the lesson rigorous?). With this template, teachers randomly select a small handful of students to periodically check for desired behaviors. For example, if a teacher wants to implement rigorous lessons, he or she identifies the desired behaviors (such as asking and answering provocative questions), selects a few random students, and then checks to see if they engage in that behavior at strategic points in the lesson.

| Student Name: | |
|---|---|
| Environment: | |

| Situations | Typical Expressions or Nonverbals |
|---|---|
| Active learning | Dates:<br>Observations: |
| Frustration when learning | Dates:<br>Observations: |
| Confusion | Dates:<br>Observations: |
| Lost or off task | Dates:<br>Observations: |

**Figure 4.5:** *Understanding a student's learning tells.*

*Visit* **go.SolutionTree.com/assessment** *for a free reproducible version of this figure.*

Student Name:

Environment:

Target Behavior:

Start Time:

Observer:

Date:

Observation period: Ten minutes, thirty-second intervals

| 9:00 | | 9:01 | | 9:02 | | 9:03 | | 9:04 | | 9:05 | | 9:06 | | 9:07 | | 9:08 | | 9:09 | |
|---|---|---|---|---|---|---|---|---|---|---|---|---|---|---|---|---|---|---|---|
| 1 | 2 | 3 | 4 | 5 | 6 | 7 | 8 | 9 | 10 | 11 | 12 | 13 | 14 | 15 | 16 | 17 | 18 | 19 | 20 |
| | | | | | | | | | | | | | | | | | | | |

Key:

+ each occurrence when target behavior occurs

− each occurrence when target behavior does not occur

**Figure 4.6:** *Interval recording observation form.*

*Visit* **go.SolutionTree.com/assessment** *for a free reproducible version of this figure.*

| | | 1 | 2 | 3 | 4 | 5 |
|---|---|---|---|---|---|---|
| Name: | | | | | | |
| Name: | | | | | | |
| Name: | | | | | | |

Environment:
Target Behavior:
Start Time:
Observer:
Date:
Observation period: Five minutes, thirty-second intervals

Key:
+ each occurrence when target behavior occurs
− each occurrence when target behavior does not occur

**Figure 4.7: *Frequency recording observation form.***

*Visit **go.SolutionTree.com/assessment** for a free reproducible version of this figure.*

# Conclusion

Observation is a significant instructional process that masterful teachers use in order to gather and interpret emerging evidence. This type of targeted observation can provide more understanding about individuals and groups of students and how a teacher might better support their learning. When teachers learn to navigate the observational process with efficiency and accuracy, they can make significant and timely instructional adaptations to smooth the learning pathway for every student.

# Pause and Ponder

Take a few moments to reflect on the following questions.

- Describe different verbal and nonverbal types of observations you currently use. To what extent are responses to these observations intentional and focused on moving students forward?

- What role do planning and assessment architecture play in using observation to make instructional maneuvers?

- Think about a lesson you have designed. Where might there be room for observation as assessment, with moments to watch what emerges?

- How could you use observations as a collaborative team to gather evidence of learning? What benefits might these types of observations have for student learning, intervention, and instructional design?

# CHAPTER 5
# MOBILIZING

*Give a man a fish, and you feed him for a day; teach him how to fish, and you feed him for a lifetime.*

—Unknown

Learners often look to their teacher for affirmation and direction. With strong instructional agility practice, the goal is to help students self-assess and self-monitor as they learn. In many classrooms, learners feel the need for this affirmation or feel paralyzed and overwhelmed regarding how to move forward. Do any of these students' comments sound familiar?

- After putting the finishing touches on her website design, Maria raises her hand and asks the teacher, "Is this right?"

- Trelle finishes the first part of the mathematics problem. Frustrated, he puts his head on the desk. As the teacher walks by, she asks him what's wrong. Trelle responds, "I don't know what to do next. I don't care."

- Jamal is working with his small group. The students are studying the water cycle and examining different scenarios, talking through how each impacts the water cycle. Each time the teacher walks by, Jamal stops, looks up, and asks, "How does this look? Are we doing it right?"

- Alex puts her pencil down and says, "I don't know where to start!" She is trying to complete a table that traces the argument of two texts.

In each case, students are struggling with the confidence to recognize where they are in their learning and the persistence to keep trying. They are heavily dependent on the teacher's affirmation and guidance. Mobilizing involves helping students develop the necessary confidence and proficiency to be able to monitor and respond to their own understanding and engagement (or lack of them).

Because learning is an active process, it stands to reason that mobilizing students as active participants in their own learning would be the most desirable result of any instructional experience. That said, most teachers quickly realize that this is often much easier said than done. The desire to have students invest in their own learning is ubiquitous, but creating the conditions and providing consistent opportunities for students to be fully invested from the start may meet with varying levels of success. Instructional maneuvers within the context of ongoing instruction provide rich opportunities to help students develop confidence and the ability to self-assess.

# The Main Idea

Creating the conditions for and nurturing the desire within students to fully invest in their own learning take time, purpose, and consistency. It doesn't happen overnight. If students have collectively been passive recipients of the instructional experience, then that's exactly what teachers will get. The simple demand that students *own their learning* falls far short of what's necessary to reverse what is often years of being on the receiving end of whatever the teacher does, says, or instructs. The most challenging aspect of mobilizing students to be instructionally agile for themselves is *how*—how can teachers create and cultivate a new kind of reality within the classroom in which students are equal participants throughout the learning process and where they are key decision makers about what comes next in their learning? The following sections outline exactly how students can participate in and own their learning.

## A Growing Body of Evidence

Evidence is emerging that supports and solidifies the idea that students can be a source of feedback and growth for themselves and for others. Researchers widely see self-assessment as a positive experience that leads to increased achievement and personal awareness (Brown & Harris, 2013), with the greatest effect being higher achievement by teaching students how to be self-regulatory about their learning (Andrade, 2010; Black & Wiliam, 1998; Hattie & Timperley, 2007; Ramdass & Zimmerman, 2008). Being more self-regulatory, including using self-assessment, draws on metacognitive competencies (Zimmerman, 2002) that have students self-observe, self-judge, self-react, self-motivate, and maintain self-control.

The research continues to show that self-assessment contributes significantly to the development of self-regulation (Andrade, Du, & Mycek, 2010; Brookhart, Andolina, Zuza, & Furman, 2004), and that self-assessment is associated with increased motivation, engagement, and efficacy (Chappuis, 2014; Munns & Woodward, 2006). The decreased dependency on the teacher as the source of all feedback (Sadler, 1989) makes feedback more readily available because students, practically speaking, have access to their own observations, their own insights, and their own feedback at any given moment.

The research on peer assessment is equally compelling, though a good portion of it focuses on college- and university-level students (Topping, 2013). Still, there is significant value in having students assess one another's work in a cooperative setting (Wiliam, 2011) to the point where some consider it one of the most important revelations to emerge from education research (Slavin, Hurley, & Chamberlain, 2003). Clearly, peer assessment has a greater number of contributing variables (for example, structure, processes, protocol, and purpose), which we discuss later in this chapter, but these variables are important in that peer assessment can be both productive and counterproductive, depending on how it's taught, how students perceive the value, the intended outcome, and what the end user should do with the information (Topping, 2013).

Student and parent perceptions of the inherent value of peer assessment can influence the process that classroom teachers have developed (Atkinson, 2003; Weaver, 1995). In many cases, teachers and parents seem to value peer assessment more than students do because the quality and usefulness of the feedback their peers provide drive students' perception (Bryant & Carless, 2010). While teachers can view peer assessment as a homogeneous process, the wide variety of iterations makes it essential that teachers (and even students) learn about both the social and academic aspects of peer assessment (van Zundert, Sluijsmans, & van Merrienboer, 2010) because students are more vulnerable and need to feel the peer assessor is trustworthy (van Gennip, Segers, & Tillema, 2009).

The bottom line is that *if* taught well and *consistently* utilized, peer assessment can contribute greatly to student achievement in ways self-assessment cannot; it is important to underscore this. In the absence of these essential factors, students actually get more inaccurate feedback from their peers (Brookhart, 2013a). Unlike self-assessment, peer assessment incorporates a social and collaborative process that inherently blends the social context with what students learn.

As established from the outset in chapter 1 (page 11), we cannot separate learning from its social context; this leaves peer assessment as a key contributor to creating and sustaining an enhanced culture of learning. In addition, peer assessment can also contribute to the growth and development of crosscurricular competencies, as peer assessment (again, unlike self-assessment) often puts students into collaborative situations where they must think critically about the work of others and communicate next steps in creative ways. We will explore this connection more deeply later in this chapter.

The point is not that one is better than the other; it is that both self-assessment and peer assessment are essential components of a culture of learning in which students can become more instructionally responsive to themselves and others. When students move from being students to becoming teachers of others, they end up learning as much as those they teach (Hattie, 2009).

## The Foundation to Mobilize

Throughout this book, we have discussed the necessary practices, processes, and prerequisites that allow teachers to respond with instructional agility; these practices, processes, and prerequisites are even more essential if teachers are to mobilize students as active assessors of their own and others' learning. Because students must learn how to self- and peer assess, teachers must first establish the conditions that make it possible for students to share in the responsibility of discerning the gap between *where they are* and *where they need to be*. If students are to mobilize on behalf of their own learning, six essentials are worth repeating in the context of transferring responsibility from teacher to student.

1. **Clear learning intentions:** Assessment begins with understanding the intended learning from any instructional experience; if this is true for teachers, then it is even truer for students. The self-assessment process begins with students' clarity about the intended outcome of the entire learning experience.

2. **Clear success criteria:** Success criteria comprise the other half of the essential pre-learning experience in which students understand *how* they demonstrate proficiency within the intended learning. Clear learning intentions articulate *what* students should learn; success criteria articulate *how* they will show that learning. Obviously, students cannot self- or peer assess if they have no sense of what success ultimately looks like.

3. **Clear interpretation of criteria:** In cases in which student responses are complex and varied, students must understand how to interpret the established success criteria. If, for example, a teacher is using a rubric to assess

writing, students must be able to draw accurate inferences between their work (or the work of others) and the established criteria. Therefore, the teacher would be wise to make time for students to practice these interpretations through the use of exemplars to help prepare them to be consistent.

4.  **A culture of wrong:** Self- and peer assessment are inherently a vulnerable experience for students. An essential prerequisite for success is to establish a classroom culture that supports being wrong. With so many inherent competitive forces around the periphery of education, it is important for teachers to formally establish an environment in which support (not ridicule) is the de facto response to needing help.

5.  **A norm of working together:** Developing a culture where working together is the norm is also essential for successful student mobilization. Teachers who randomly—and occasionally—put students in situations to self- and peer assess will predictably be disappointed with the limited (or lack of) results. The more that teachers set students up to practice their own mobilizing efforts, the less foreign these efforts seem. Self- and peer assessment take practice, so establishing this norm of collective work has a tremendous payoff.

6.  **Some student proficiency:** Feedback is most effective when it addresses at least a partial understanding of the intended learning, which means feedback is not often helpful for those who have no understanding of the learning; this is also true for student mobilization. The comparison between *where they are* and *where they need to be* assumes they are at least *somewhere* along their path of learning. When self- and peer assessment come too soon in the learning process, students may not have enough sophistication to discern their (or others') gaps and, more important, may not have enough sophistication to provide any meaningful advice. The timing of self- and peer assessment can play a large role in the success or failure of the process to enhance student achievement.

While these universal prerequisites are essential, assessment is contextually sensitive and nuanced, which means teachers must pay attention to the unique conditions and circumstances that increase the likelihood of a productive effort to mobilize students as owners of their own learning. In this case, teachers are instructionally agile, as they recognize when students need support and instruction in order to facilitate achieving more independence in moving their learning forward.

## Potential Limitations

The research has been clear for some time that the most effective students are those who self-regulate their learning (Butler & Winne, 1995). However, no matter how proficient and insightful a student might be in recognizing his or her own strengths and deficiencies, all self-assessments are imperfect (Brown & Harris, 2013). Accuracy is a constant concern, which means teachers can never completely withdraw from the self-assessment process. Mobilizing students has nothing to do with teachers relinquishing control or influence; it's about raising students to a level at which they authentically feel they can contribute to their own learning experiences. But teachers must remain involved, though their role will shift to one of oversight rather than initial assessment. The potential flaws in self-assessment are not a reason to ignore the process; rather, they serve as a reminder that students still need teachers to ensure the accuracy of their initial determinations.

David Dunning, Chip Heath, and Jerry M. Suls (2004) identify the following four potential flaws or limitations to the self-assessment process. These limitations do not describe only students; they apply to all human beings.

1.  **The tendency for humans to be unrealistically optimistic:** Students may underplay how long their path to proficiency is or underestimate the amount of work necessary to reach the next level. Here teachers would need to make sure students have a realistic view of what it takes to keep learning.

2.  **The tendency for humans to believe they are above average:** Students, especially those who have yet to reach a minimal level of proficiency, may believe the quality of their work or performance is greater than it is. Very few people (let alone students) are willing to admit they are below average at anything critical or crucial. There are below-average drivers, doctors, lawyers, teachers, mechanics, friends, and more, and yet most are unwilling to admit it. The need to enhance self-worth may be a contributing factor (Saavedra & Kwun, 1993). Accuracy with self-assessment increases with age as well as academic proficiency (Brown & Harris, 2013). In other words, older students and more proficient students will self-assess more accurately.

3.  **The tendency for humans to neglect crucial information:** Students may inadvertently or intentionally ignore certain unfavorable performance indicators that they actually should use to assess their own work. Inadvertently ignoring certain indicators could reveal a lack of clarity on the success criteria; intentionally ignoring certain performance indicators would reveal a dishonest approach to self-assessment.

4.  **The tendency for humans to have deficits in their information:** Students' lack of clarity on success criteria may result in them simply not knowing what to look for in their own work. This reinforces the notion that students need at least a minimal level of proficiency in order to accurately assess their own work.

Dunning et al. (2004) point out that there can be many issues related to the accuracy of self-assessment; those not competent within a domain are likely not aware of their lack of competence. This only compounds the potential self-assessment inaccuracies. Again, this is not to suggest that self-assessment is not a worthwhile assessment process—*it is*. It just means teachers cannot back away from the process and assume students can do it for themselves.

The limitation of peer assessment is the external dependency on students to accurately assess others' work. All the potential limitations of self-assessment are applicable on the front end of the peer-assessment process (for example, clear criteria and accurate interpretation), but there are additional potential issues on the back end. Unlike self-assessment, peer assessment relies on the peer assessor clearly articulating an accurate and applicable pathway forward. Even if the peer assessor accurately assesses another's work, the process can unravel if he or she does not clearly articulate the path forward with a level of specificity that allows an actionable, agile response. When assessing peers, students must understand how to give one another feedback, which adds another contributing variable to the success or limitations of the process.

Peer assessment is more readily available (there is only one teacher but a classroom full of students), but it obviously may not be as reliable. Like most strategies, when taught and executed well, peer assessment provides a powerful learning experience for the assessor and his or her subject; when executed poorly, it can be a counterproductive experience that takes away more than it adds to the learning.

## Connections to Other Tenets

Mobilizing students to be instructionally agile on their own behalf is primarily anchored in the *student investment* tenet; students who are invested in their learning are more likely to mobilize in response to their assessment results. The ultimate test of any culture of learning is how invested students are in the process from start to finish. Students who are invested understand the intended learning, have clarity on success criteria, identify the discrepancy between where they are and where they need to be, articulate their own next steps toward proficiency, and believe that their potential success is limitless. Instructionally agile students must be invested and will significantly contribute to their own learning trajectory. When invested students have all the tools for accurate self-assessment, they are empowered to activate their own learning process in meaningful ways. They mobilize their learning journey with intention and a focused goal.

Again, the art of instructional agility is to *plan with precision* so one can *respond with agility*. All of the assessment tenets feed the process of mobilizing students to maximize their opportunities so they can maintain their learning momentum. When students are clear on the assessment purpose, they know whether the self- or peer assessment should be quantitative or qualitative. Precision with assessment architecture affords teachers the opportunity to purposefully build in mobilizing opportunities for students. This also requires due attention to accurate interpretation, which means teachers must establish clear criteria and communicate to students what proficiency looks like, especially when assessment hinges on accurate inferences by student assessors.

The result of mobilizing students within the self- and peer assessment processes should be effectively communicating results (to themselves or others) to trigger further learning. For teachers, effective feedback is any feedback that triggers a productive learning response from students; the same holds true for students, only they are triggering productive responses within themselves or others. In essence, all assessment practices and processes ideally lead to investment and, consequently, student mobilization. The synergy of the assessment tenets develops a culture of learning in which students themselves invest in carving their own path to proficiency.

# Mobilizing in Action

Mobilizing students to be instructionally agile is both simple and complex. It's simple in that the processes and strategies are not conceptually complicated, but it's complex because consistently using those practices and processes requires a level of intentionality that isn't always easy to sustain. Likewise, there are multitudes of ways that students can mobilize, as outlined in the following sections.

## Options for Self-Assessment

Some educators view self-assessment and peer assessment as universal, singular processes that look the same in every classroom when, in fact, there are a multitude of assessment options and, therefore, questions teachers must answer as they pursue each approach to mobilizing students. With self-assessment, teachers must address the following key questions as they shape the self-assessment process.

- Is it qualitative?
- Is it quantitative?
- Is it both?
- Is it metacognitive?
- Is it all three?

## Is It Qualitative?

Qualitative self-assessment is arguably the most common form of self-assessment—students use the success criteria to specifically describe their own next steps in addressing the gap between where they are and where they need to be. It is the truest type of formative assessment in which students pursue the specific details of how to improve within the specific aspects of quality.

Within qualitative feedback, the additional question arises of whether the self-assessment should balance both strengths and areas in need of improvement, or whether it should pinpoint one or the other. The orthodoxy of feedback processes, even when a learner is engaged in self-feedback, would suggest it be balanced. However, there may be times when students focus only on strengths or only on areas in need of improvement. At first, teachers might ask novice students to identify areas of strength in order to grow their efficacy with both the intended learning and the process of self-assessment. Proficient students whose efficacy is high may simply focus exclusively on those aspects requiring more attention.

## Is It Quantitative?

With quantitative self-assessment, rather than looking for specificity, students make an overall judgment of quality via the success criteria. Though it may not contribute to a report card grade, students make a holistic judgment based on the totality of the criteria. While it certainly involves less description, the quantitative process asks students to replicate the process their teachers use within the summative purpose of assessment. If students review quantitative data by learning target, which indicates a certain level of proficiency, there is a more targeted opportunity to self-assess. However, the limitations of holistic judgments on what specific aspects contributed to proficiency can make specific, improvement-focused responses more challenging.

## Is It Both?

At times, a teacher might ask students to describe with specificity their next steps and determine an overall level or score. Of course, the most important facet of this process is still the pursuit of higher proficiency, so we must consider the potential negative impact that scores (even initial scores) can have on learning. What's clear in the research is that the existence of levels and scores can interfere with student willingness to keep learning, so if students accurately determine a satisfactory level or score, they may not pursue the necessary improvements. If students settle (and subsequently ignore their own feedback), then the process was pointless. If, however, students use their own feedback to improve the quality of their work, then the existence of a level or score is no issue.

## Is It Metacognitive?

At times, teachers might ask students to self-assess and reflect on their own cognitive processes as students instead of on the quality of their work. This introspective reflection is valuable as students mobilize and invest in their learning. They might ask, "What part of the process helped me learn? Where did I get bogged down or frustrated? What did I do when I got frustrated or didn't know what to do?" These kinds of questions guide students to begin to understand how they learn best.

## Is It All Three?

Though rare, and arguably unfocused, this process has students make an overall judgment, describe their own next steps in learning, and reflect on the process of producing the end product or demonstration. Provided the process is clear, students can combine all three types of self-assessment, which could certainly create an enriching self-assessment process.

# Options for Peer Assessment

In addition to the qualitative, quantitative, and metacognitive options, mobilizing students with peer-to-peer processes has additional options and iterations that teachers can tailor to the age and sophistication of the students, as well as the content and processes they are assessing. The same prerequisites (clear interpretation of learning intentions and success criteria) are necessary, however, it is also necessary to teach students *how* to give one another feedback in ways that promote a willingness to improve. (We will explore this issue of communication later in this chapter.) When mobilizing students with peer-to-peer experiences, teachers need to at least consider the following questions if they are going to maximize the results of this collective experience.

- Is it a one-way, two-way, or group experience?
- Is the subsequent action immediate or delayed?
- Are pairings random or intentional?
- Is it a one-time or long-term connection?
- Is it face to face or virtual?

## Is It a One-Way, Two-Way, or Group Experience?

In some cases, peer-to-peer feedback may flow in one direction; that is, students themselves receive feedback from one peer while providing feedback to a different peer. In other cases, the process may be reciprocal, with students partnering with the intent to give each other feedback. The process might also be group based, such that each student provides feedback to each group member.

## Is the Subsequent Action Immediate or Delayed?

While the most productive feedback is typically immediately actionable, there may be times when peer-to-peer feedback informs a learner's next steps at a later date. Teachers may anchor this decision on the collective level of proficiency—students at high levels of proficiency may have the capacity to transfer peer feedback from one session to another, while novice students will likely benefit from taking more immediate action upon receiving others' advice.

## Are Pairings Random or Intentional?

The choice between random or intentional pairings has much to do with what outcome of the process the teacher intends. In some cases (such as writing), the teacher may intentionally create homogenous pairings to allow students at similar levels of proficiency to mobilize one another into action; heterogeneous pairings may result in a one-way conversation in which a strong writer has a lot to say to the novice writer, but the novice writer has little to offer in return. In other cases (such as debating the merits of a current government policy), heterogeneous pairings may allow for diverse perspectives and, maybe, multicultural or multi-economic perspectives. One is not inherently better than the other. The point is that this advanced decision influences the success of the process on the back end. The question of *random* versus *intentional* is equally applicable in group settings.

## Is It a One-Time or Long-Term Connection?

With isolated or finite tasks, the pairings (or groupings) may be a one-time connection for the purpose of mobilizing students' collective efforts to keep learning, while in other cases, creating a long-term connection has advantages. Where a standard is skill based and runs longitudinally through a course from start to finish (for example, Socratic seminars or argumentative writing), it may be beneficial to create pairings or groupings that last throughout the course duration.

At best, this long-term relationship would create efficiency and effectiveness by developing familiarity with both the nuances of how to demonstrate proficiency as well as the personal connection. In other words, students would eventually become familiar with personal idiosyncrasies both in and out of learning as well as with underlying or inferred approaches to demonstrating that learning. Both *one-time* and *long-term connections* can occur simultaneously with, for example, content standards being finite and skill-based standards being long term.

## Is It Face to Face or Virtual?

The obvious iteration of peer-to-peer mobilization is face to face, but technology allows for feedback to come virtually from anywhere across a country or around the world. If students upload work samples, videos, audio recordings, or other performances to a digital platform, they can solicit feedback from anywhere. A student who records an original piece of music could upload it to solicit both positive comments and constructive suggestions from anyone willing to take the time to listen. Like anything online, it is important for teachers to monitor and possibly limit access, especially for elementary students for whom online communication can be counterproductive and mean spirited. That said, the potential for global feedback is limitless in ideal conditions.

## The Four Cs

An additional outcome of mobilizing students within the self- and peer assessment processes is the direct connection it provides to teaching crosscurricular competencies (also known as 21st century skills or the four Cs). The four Cs—*critical thinking, creativity, collaboration*, and *communication* (Kay & Greenhill, 2013; Partnership for 21st Century Skills, 2011)—are well embedded within the mobilizing processes we have discussed so far. And while it would be an overreach to suggest student automaticity with the four Cs, it is not a stretch to suggest that with some intentionality, teachers can highlight the ways students can learn these important skills as they take on the realities facing them in adulthood. Again, it is important to recognize that the connection between mobilizing students and the four Cs must be intentional and explicit.

### Critical Thinking

The process of assessing in and of itself is a critical-thinking skill, especially when the assessment involves analyzing, making inferences, comparing, or critiquing a performance that is open to interpretation against the established criteria. When students self-assess their proficiency with any skill (such as serving a volleyball) they must analyze their own performance against the established criteria and mobilize on behalf of themselves to improve their ability to perform the skill. The critical-thinking skills consist of *how* students will analyze their own performances while the directions they provide to themselves create the subsequent actions. Peer assessment creates a similar dynamic.

As well, if mobilizing is *quantitative*, then teachers ask students—whether self- or peer assessing—to *synthesize* criteria while *analyzing* performances to make an overall judgment, both of which are critical thinking processes. The more established a teacher or school's efforts are toward developing the four Cs within students, the greater the connection between student mobilization and important 21st century skills, or crosscurricular competencies.

## Creativity

Synthesis requires both critical and creative thinking. There is an art to both summarizing and providing clear directions on what's next, especially in situations in which the receiving student is not as confident or has a limited view of what proficiency looks like. Feedback is more than just telling it like it is; it requires discretion and some creativity to trigger predictive responses within oneself or other students. Again, the connection to creativity is admittedly limited, but it does exist, and, with purpose, teachers can devise yet another opportunity for students to realize how creativity is inherent in so many of today's common practices.

## Collaboration

Peer assessment is inherent collaboration in learning. Whether reciprocal or group based, peer assessment provides an obvious opportunity to teach and reinforce skills and behaviors that enhance any collaborative effort. Active listening, healthy debate, coming to consensus, and conflict resolution are but a few of the characteristics of effective collaboration embedded in the peer assessment process. If, for example, multiple sources provide peer feedback, they may disagree on what's next for the student, which would lead to some discussion and debate about how best to mobilize the student going forward. Reciprocal exercises certainly require some collaboration, but the group-based exercises provide overt and ample opportunities for teachers to use the processes of collaboration to mobilize students.

## Communication

The connection between mobilization and communication is, of course, very strong. Whether it is articulating one's own next steps or the next steps of others, mindfulness of the skills of effective communication is essential. Besides the obvious need to communicate in a face-to-face, reciprocal exercise, there are other mobilization iterations that require some unique attention to communication. If the feedback is online, then students must pay attention to word choice and inferred tone, as written feedback lacks the nonverbal cues that facilitate face-to-face communication. Culture might also be a factor, especially when online peer feedback is more global (feedback can come from around the world); attention to cultural norms of collaboration is necessary. Even within the same country, there are undoubtedly many multicultural norms to navigate. As always, the degree of attention teachers give to the connection undoubtedly equals the degree of awareness students have while mobilizing others' efforts to improve.

We are describing the ways in which teaching and learning the four Cs are embedded within the mobilizing processes to help highlight the opportunities that already exist. Teachers can mistakenly view the instruction and development of the four Cs as a separate, stand-alone process that many simply don't have time for. The truth is that many instructional processes align nicely with teaching the four Cs.

In most cases, teachers need intentionality and a little effort to create congruent opportunities for students to grow in several areas simultaneously. Defining the success criteria of these four Cs and designing tasks and activities in which students engage provide rich opportunities for teachers to mobilize students as resources for themselves and their peers. Instructional agility includes the ability of teachers to set up classroom culture and its routines in order to realize the power and promise of peer and self-assessment.

## Self-Regulation

Mobilizing students to be instructionally agile for themselves is part of the larger picture of improving self-regulation. Self-regulation is when students set goals and then take action cognitively, behaviorally, and affectively toward reaching those goals (Zimmerman & Schunk, 2011). Addressing both student affect and behavior serves as an essential reminder that educators teach the *whole child*.

The self-regulatory process includes incorporating practices that consider student efficacy, interest, and outcome expectations. Not only can students monitor their learning, they can be aware of how they learn before, during, and after any instructional processes (that is, metacognition). Most researchers view self-regulation as a cyclical process of interrelated phases (Brookhart, 2013a). While Barry J. Zimmerman (2011) articulates the self-regulation of learning as three phases (forethought, performance, and reflection), Paul R. Pintrich and Akane Zusho (2002) identify four: (1) forethought, (2) monitoring, (3) control, and (4) reflection. While each model—and others—may vary in the minutiae, they all distinguish among before-, during-, and after-learning processes.

During the *forethought* phase, students would not only consider what teachers ask of them academically but also reflect on their levels of efficacy, interest, and motivation toward completing the task at hand. During the learning (*monitor* and *control*), students monitor the quality of their work and reflect on how they are producing the work (strategies and behaviors). After learning, students evaluate the quality of their own or others' work as well as *reflect* on their level of satisfaction with what they produced and how they produced it. This results in another goal-setting opportunity and a subsequent move back to the forethought phase. The main idea is that a teacher's efforts to mobilize students are a seamless way to develop self-regulatory behavior.

# Strategies and Tools

While it isn't possible to explore every possible strategy or iteration that makes student mobilization possible, this section offers some strategies and tools to make mobilizing more likely.

## Strategy 1: Co-Construct Success Criteria

When students have a clear understanding of both learning intentions and success criteria, it is more possible for them to mobilize on behalf of themselves. Students can hit any target they can see (Stiggins, 2008). They make decisions at every point along their learning continuums; however, not every decision they make is necessarily on point or feeds their advancement to proficiency, especially when they base their decisions on an incomplete or faulty understanding of the learning outcomes.

Once teachers clarify the intended learning outcomes, they can deepen students' understanding of what successfully achieving that outcome looks like by involving them in constructing the success criteria. As Anne Davies (2007) writes, "When we involve learners in co-constructing criteria, they grasp important ideas more readily because they are translating expectations into language that they understand" (p. 39).

Most students have some idea of what quality work looks like, even if their views are incomplete or faulty in some areas. Involving students in co-constructing criteria has nothing to do with teachers relinquishing any control or influence; teachers must still be the final arbiters of the criteria. However, by co-constructing criteria, teachers put students in a position where they must consider the end result and the possible iterations of what success looks like. Co-constructing criteria can also serve as a formative assessment strategy because through that process, the teacher learns what students know and don't know about the task, skill, or process at hand.

Kathleen Gregory, Caren Cameron, and Anne Davies (1997) outline a simple four-step process teachers can use to co-construct criteria with students.

1. **Brainstorm:** Brainstorm a list of ideas of what quality work looks like. Teachers often use a question or prompt to elicit ideas from students. A few possibilities include the following: *What does quality writing look like, sound like, and feel like? What are the important aspects of a quality science lab report? What does a great speech sound like?* The point is to prompt students to put into their own words what it will be like to succeed; the teacher ensures that, in most cases, they describe quality in generic terms, which allows the criteria to apply across multiple demonstrations.

2.  **Sort, group, and label:** Students then sort and group the ideas into logical clusters. They label these clusters with generic headings that organize the criteria. For example, they may organize all the ideas for *what makes a great speech* into categories such as *explanation of ideas, organization, supporting materials, integration of technology, nonverbal actions,* and *voice.*

3.  **Make a T-chart:** The learning demonstration's cognitive complexity dictates how detailed the criteria are, but in any event, students should organize groupings into a chart that clearly articulates what success looks like. The left side of the chart lists the cluster labels, while the right side lists students' brainstormed ideas.

4.  **Use the criteria to guide the work:** Ideally, the teacher posts the T-chart or otherwise makes it accessible to students so they can, while producing their work, consistently refer back to the chart to check where they are against where they need to be.

While there are few steps, it is important that teachers not rush the process to provide ample time for students to reflect on what proficiency looks like. As well, teachers may develop a rubric with greater specificity from the established criteria. Sharing that with students would eventually be beneficial, but in the early stages it may be advantageous to keep the explanation of the criteria as simple as possible by simply articulating *here's what success looks like* without clouding the process with levels of success.

## Strategy 2: Practice With Exemplars

On occasion, students have little to no idea what success looks like, so the teacher might begin the co-constructing process by presenting exemplars. But in most cases, exemplars would follow the co-constructing process. Exemplars bring the criteria to life and provide students with a clear sense of what strong and weak work looks like. This requires a little planning on the teachers' part because gathering anonymous samples may take some time; they often come from previous years' demonstrations. Once the teacher has established the criteria and possibly developed a quality rubric, students can use a collaborative process to practice with exemplars until their view of quality aligns with the teachers.

The following six-step process is one effective way to teach criteria through the use of exemplars.

1.  **Teacher shares the exemplar:** Read, show, demonstrate, or present exemplars through the means of video.

2. **Students independently assess:** Using the established criteria, students assess the exemplar on the aspects of quality that the criteria have established.

3. **Students share with their small group:** Within a small group (for example, four students), each student shares his or her individual perspective on the exemplar.

4. **Groups establish consensus:** After all students have shared, each group attempts to come to consensus on the exemplar's proficiency level.

5. **Class engages in a discussion:** Each group shares its determined proficiency level for the exemplar, the teacher shares the actual level, and a discussion ensues (assuming some discrepancy between a few students and the teacher).

6. **The process repeats:** Repeat the process as many times as necessary so students deeply understand the success criteria.

There are two aspects of using exemplars that teachers should consider. They should make clear that *duplicating* the exemplar is not the goal; students should strive to *replicate* the criteria. Teachers should advise students against simply copying what classmates have done in the past. As well, teachers should thoughtfully choose the exemplars. While it is true that some students produce work that is far superior to the expected grade-level standards, using these demonstrations as exemplars could be counterproductive for students whose efficacy is fragile. Exemplars should solidly reflect the criteria but should also feel attainable to the maximum number of students.

## Strategy 3: Set Goals

Once students are clear on the learning intentions and success criteria, they can look inward and determine what goals they have moving forward. According to Hattie (2009), "Goals have a self-energizing effect if they are appropriately challenging for the learner, as they can motivate the learners to exert effort in line with the difficulty or demands of the goal" (p. 164). Hattie (2009) specifically encourages difficult goals over *do your best* goals because "anything you do can be defined as your best" (p. 164); D. Royce Sadler (1989) suggests that *do your best* goals are not that much more effective than having no goals at all.

Students' current standing determines how independently they can set goals and know which aspects of their learning need attention. Figure 5.1 (page 116) provides an example of a goal-setting form or process students can use to set challenging goals. They can use the form as-is or tailor it to suit the given situation or circumstance.

| Framing Question | Response |
|---|---|
| What is the learning intention? | |
| What are the success criteria? | |
| Where are you now in relation to the intended learning? | |
| What evidence do you have to support determining your current status? | |

My challenging goal is _____.
My plan to reach my goal is _____.
I intend to reach my goal by this date: _____.
If I need help, I will _____.

**Figure 5.1:** *Goal-setting form.*

*Visit go.SolutionTree.com/assessment for a free reproducible version of this figure.*

There are countless ways in which teachers can engage students in goal-setting exercises. The point is to have them set challenging goals that are specifically related to their location on the path to proficiency, enabling them to mobilize efficiently. Precision in design allows for maximum flexibility in response, so the more teachers provide opportunities for students to prepare in advance of self- and peer assessment, the greater chance there is of maximizing the intended results of the process on the back end.

## Strategy 4: Self-Assess

The possible iterations of self- and peer assessment are endless. The strategies we present in this section offer a menu of options. However, teachers shouldn't feel restricted by this information; the only restriction is a teacher's own imagination of what's possible.

Following are a few possibilities for how teachers can mobilize students to invest in their own learning.

- **Qualitative self-assessment:** Students use the criteria—which teachers often articulate in rubric form—to assess themselves. They highlight the applicable boxes within each aspect of quality. They can also do this orally by demonstrating proficiency through a performance (for example, shooting a basketball in physical education). Students could articulate their view of specific aspects of the performance (for example, the specific elements of shooting a basketball, such as follow-through and elbow position) based on the established criteria. The point is to have students *drill down* to the specific areas of strength and those areas needing improvement.

- **Quantitative self-assessment:** Students make an overall judgment of quality. This is when students synthesize criteria to make an overall determination (for example, a student might say, "Overall, I'm a 3 or proficient when it comes to argumentative writing"). This judgment is not to factor into actual grades, but it does put students in a position to experience firsthand how the teacher will grade them.

- **Strength-based self-assessment:** Students only identify areas of strength within their performances or demonstrations. The focus here is to build hope and efficacy within the specific performance, especially for novices or beginners.

- **Improvement-based self-assessment:** Students only identify areas needing improvement within their performances or demonstrations. The focus here is on students who are performing at a proficient or advanced level and whose hope and efficacy about success are not in question. Identifying strengths is never wrong, but this approach is more efficient.

## Strategy 5: Assess Peers

Teachers can use all the self-assessment approaches we identify here with peer assessment as well. Following are a few possibilities for how teachers can organize students to invest and mobilize on behalf of one another.

- **Reciprocal, qualitative, intentional pairings:** Teachers organize students into homogenous pairings in which they work with peers at the same proficiency level to describe for one another how each can improve the quality of his or her work.

- **Group-based, qualitative, random groupings:** Teachers randomly assign students to groups to provide feedback to each other. With tangible demonstrations (such as writing), each student assesses each demonstration and provides feedback on it. For performances (such as speaking in a foreign language), each student could take turns performing, and other group members can provide feedback simultaneously. The advantage here is that mixed-ability groups allow students who are less proficient to see firsthand what proficiency looks like. Proficient students get the opportunity to teach, which also deepens understanding.

- **Long-term, intentional pairings:** Teachers intentionally pair students with partners they will work with for a long period of time. These pairings could include students who already have mutual trust and aren't afraid to be vulnerable with one another. It is also possible to create more content-driven pairings (for example, two students who enjoy reading the same genre) or process-driven pairings (for example, peer editing partners). The advantage here is that a long-term relationship develops so the peer-assessment process becomes more seamless and embedded. With increased trust comes increased willingness to be vulnerable, leading to more accurate feedback and revision.

- **Long-term, intentional groupings:** Teachers intentionally group students with a long-term focus, allowing the group members to mutually support and push one another. For example, in physical education, students with similar fitness goals work collectively to support one another; in world languages, students work with peers at similar levels of fluency. The intent here is for each student to equally contribute to mobilizing others.

- **Online global groupings:** Students upload a digital copy of their work to a personal blog site or web page and ask for feedback in the form of comments. This could be a closed opportunity, with access restricted only to certain classrooms from across a school, district, state, country, or the world. This would prevent and control the unsolicited, negative, counterproductive feedback that characterizes some online sites. The site could be wide open, but again, teachers would have to closely moderate the contents to permit only purposeful, positive, and constructive comments. While labor intensive, this maximizes the potential sources of feedback for students.

The possibilities are endless. The key for teachers is to be clear on what they hope students are able to accomplish within the peer-assessment process so they can create the optimal conditions for students to mobilize their own and others' learning.

## Strategy 6: Respond to Assessments

After the process is complete—whether self- or peer assessment—the best-case scenario is that students mobilize to improve on their current standing. Following are a few possibilities for how teachers can organize students to respond to their own or others' assessments of their demonstration of learning.

- **Use a three-part reflection:** Teachers ask students to reflect on three aspects of their learning process: (1) achievement, (2) learning habits, and (3) growth. Figure 5.2 shows an example of a reflection form students can use. Each of these questions could also serve as a stand-alone strategy.

---

Now that our peer-assessment process is complete, answer the following three questions to plan your next steps.

1. Did you achieve the goal you set for yourself in advance of the learning? If so, what specifically did you accomplish? If not, where did your performance fall short?

2. While you were working, did you notice any improvement in your habits of learning? Describe the differences you noticed in how you learn.

3. In what specific areas of achievement have you grown? You could start by answering the following prompt.

I used to _____, but now I _____.

---

**Figure 5.2: Three-part reflection form.**

*Visit **go.SolutionTree.com/assessment** for a free reproducible version of this figure.*

- **Set new goals:** After examining their current performance, teachers ask students to re-examine their goals in light of the new information they've received. Students could be asked the following questions.

  - "If you're satisfied with your performance, what new goal will you set for yourself, and how do you plan to achieve that goal?"

  - "If you're dissatisfied with your performance, is there anything you could do differently to ensure that you achieve your goal?"

- **Develop a learning plan:** Students can examine their performances through the lens of what they did well, where they made mistakes, and what additional learning they need to undertake. This allows students to take the feedback from themselves (or others) and organize it into a plan for going forward. Figure 5.3 (page 120) is an example of a short form that students could use to develop this plan.

| |
|---|
| Areas of learning in which I am really strong: |
| Areas of learning in which I know what to do, but keep making mistakes that prevent me from being strong: |
| Areas of learning in which I need more instruction: |
| My plan to stop making the same mistakes: |
| My plan to learn what I still need to learn (and who can help me): |

**Figure 5.3: *Learning plan.***

Visit **go.SolutionTree.com/assessment** *for a free reproducible version of this figure.*

# Conclusion

In the end, the processes of self- and peer assessment are only effective if they lead students to take action. Going through the processes is good, but reacting to the processes and the subsequent information they provide is better. Teachers who intentionally plan to provide students with opportunities to mobilize during the *design, interpretation,* and *response* phases are more likely to create the conditions—and routines—that allow students to be instructionally agile for themselves and others.

The critical piece to mobilizing students throughout the assessment process is to ensure that sound assessment practices and processes are in place in the classroom. All the practices students experience via the teacher (for example, clear learning goals, success criteria, interpretation, feedback, and response) help students act within those routines with support, and eventually on their own. Instructional agility is not just for teachers; mobilizing is an intentional practice to help students self-regulate and, in turn, succeed. It is this commitment that leads teachers to develop a culture of learning and mobilizing as a way of becoming instructionally agile.

# Pause and Ponder

Take a few moments to reflect on the following questions.

- Of the six aspects that lay the foundation for mobilizing students (clear learning intentions, clear success criteria, clear interpretation of criteria, a culture of wrong, a norm of working together, and some student proficiency), which do you think is an area of strength in your classroom? Which might need a little more attention? Explain.

- Of the four potential limitations of self-assessment (being unrealistically optimistic, believing oneself to be above average, neglecting crucial information, and having deficits in information), which is the most common among your students when they self-assess?

- Describe your most successful experiences with mobilizing students on behalf of their own learning through self-assessment. Why do you think it has been so successful?

- Describe your least successful experiences with mobilizing students on behalf of their own learning through self-assessment. If you could go back, what would you do to change that experience to make it more successful? Is it a strategy you would like to return to? Explain.

# CHAPTER 6
# PRACTICING

*Take chances, make mistakes. That's how you grow. . . .*
*You have to fail in order to practice being brave.*

—Mary Tyler Moore

Practice is important. Experts in any field—even those who are naturally gifted—will say they can never get enough practice on their road to perfection. Pablo Casals, the world's foremost cellist in the late 1950s, performed at the United Nations when he was eighty-one years old. Asked at that time why he continued to practice four to five hours a day, Casals replied, "Because I think I am making progress" (Quote Investigator, n.d.). And he is not alone in that perspective.

NBA star Michael Jordan said:

> I've missed more than nine thousand shots in my career. I've lost almost three hundred games. Twenty-six times I've been trusted to take the game winning shot—and missed. I've failed over and over and over again in my life. That is why I succeed. (Richardson, 2004, p. 72)

The mantra of failure as a critical aspect of success works in business as well. Henry Ford and Samuel Crowther (1922) created the notion that failure is the opportunity to begin again more intelligently. Ted W. Engstrom, humanitarian leader and author, once stated, "We must expect to fail, but fail in a learning posture, determined not to repeat the mistakes, and to maximize the benefits from what is learned in the process." From long ago to modern day and across all industries, people value practice and the experience of failure as important components of the learning process.

Students must maintain a growth mindset, otherwise, all the practice in the world will not support the desired change. Carol Dweck (2006) points out that students with a growth mindset are willing to take risks, recognize mistakes as learning opportunities rather than failures, and engage their efforts to reduce the discrepancy between where they currently are and where they would like to be in their learning progress. They are also willing to fail. Failing often and failing well involve risk taking—a learning-based behavior that shouldn't be problematic in a genuine learning environment.

Certain practices can influence the development of a growth mindset, including unintentionally shutting it down. When teachers record failure as a quantitative mark in the gradebook, it can have a negative effect on students' mindset. Students may avoid challenging tasks for fear of failure and a low grade. If teachers average grades together, especially within the same standard, any low grade can be exponentially more difficult to overcome. When teachers use points or grades on everything students do, it can be hard for students to make connections between working hard and learning more.

Practice doesn't make perfect; instead, practice makes *permanent* (Wolfe, 2010). In *Practice Perfect*, author Dan Heath writes, "The mere fact of doing something repeatedly does not help us improve. What we need is practice—real practice, not mere repetition" (Lemov, Woolway, & Yezzi, 2012, p. 10). Teachers often deem repetition and drilling as forms of practice; however, both offer but a shadow of the truly robust cognitive and sometimes emotional and physical commitment someone must apply when genuinely trying to improve. In order for practice to work, students must exhibit a high degree of purposefulness and mindfulness as they monitor personal progress:

> You have to be able, on your own, to size up when to use what you previously learned, i.e., analyze the challenge, and judge what to do, mindful of a repertoire of prior learning; then, implement a purposeful move, and assess its effect. (Wiggins, 2013)

If practice is to serve its purpose in the classroom, then teachers cannot simply require students to repeat or drill on key details and skills and continually record the results; this method simply will not cultivate the required growth mindset.

# The Main Idea

Students must be able to practice to achieve proficiency with new learning. Under the right two conditions, practice is a powerful learning tool. The first condition enables students to make mistakes; the second includes reflecting on what works and what doesn't. Ultimately, with these conditions in place, students persist until they achieve mastery. The process requires reflection and commitment, along with customization and autonomy. Each student focuses on what he or she needs and makes strategic decisions about what comes next in the learning. This runs counter to the common classroom practice of assigning the same practice to all students and then scoring all practice work. This means that teachers may need to make dramatic changes in the way they manage their classrooms to maximize the potential of practice.

Equally important, practice provides teachers with the required emerging evidence they need to demonstrate agility during instruction. The data revealed from the evidence provide both teachers and students the necessary information to make informed decisions about what comes next in the instructional process. Practice work can happen within the classroom, during instruction, or beyond class time at home. *Where* the work happens is not important; it's more important that teachers analyze evidence students produce through practice, and students act on the feedback.

## Practice in the Classroom

Often, teachers can manage practice in class: "Guided instruction requires that teachers consider what the student knows and what the student still needs to know. It's part of a comprehensive framework for instruction that includes establishing purpose and modeling, productive group work, and independent learning tasks" (Fisher & Frey, 2010, p. 116). During the instructional phases, teachers engage students in trying their hand at new learning. Typically, teachers engage in a process of gradual release of responsibility, moving from *I do* to *we do* to *you do*. Gradual release allows the teacher to gently pass the baton to students—from the teacher owning the learning to individual students owning the learning (Fisher & Frey, 2010). Practice provides the evidence for teachers and students to see what each student takes from instruction.

Within the framework of the lesson itself, teachers can manage in-class practice within the whole group, in small groups, and by individual students. When practice is *collaborative* (all or some students working together), teachers can capitalize on helping students diagnose common mistakes, errors, or misconceptions that may occur. However, collaborative practice can never offer sufficient evidence of an individual student's understanding.

Fisher and Frey (2010) state:

> With whole-class guided instruction, the questions have to be posed in such a way that each student is accountable for responding. This can be accomplished with personal dry erase boards, partner conversations, audience-response systems, thumbs up/down, and a host of other instructional routines. (p. 117)

It's important for teachers to also gather sample student responses in order to understand each student's progress on the learning expectations. No matter who generates the work—groups or individuals—the review processes that follow practice must lead to clarity regarding next steps for each student.

## Analysis and Feedback

*All* practice requires feedback. Marks (for example, ✓), scores (12/15), or grades (B–) do not provide students with the necessary information and feedback to make informed instructional decisions (Chappuis, 2014; Hattie, 2009; O'Connor, 2011; Schimmer, 2016). Leadership expert and author Rick Tate (as cited in Blanchard, 2015) calls feedback "the breakfast of champions." It is only helpful when it feeds forward. All students should know as much about their personal strengths following an assessment as they do about their weaknesses. Success and intervention feedback are necessary for every student following every assessment (Chappuis, 2014). With care, teachers can use practice artifacts to provide feedback in a manner that supports learning for all students, simultaneously. Homework can be an effective source for feedback, but it must be done in an environment free of judgment, allowing students to grow from their mistakes.

### Safety and Judgment

To begin, it's important to create a culture of safety in which teachers and students withhold judgment, view mistakes as opportunities, and employ discussions about error solely to help students identify the stumbling blocks currently holding them back from achieving their desired goals. All practice should conclude with teacher analysis of the results to inform next steps. Teachers and students must begin to identify the common mistakes, misconceptions, and errors that occur before the teacher can expect each student to diagnose his or her own unique patterns of inaccuracy. The process requires corrective action early in the process; otherwise, mistakes, misconceptions, and errors can lead to tremendous learning hurdles later on.

If a student has provided prior or additional evidence to suggest he or she truly understands the question or concept at hand, the teacher might determine that an inaccurate answer on an assessment is a mistake. Mistakes can be a result of reading errors (skipping key words), misunderstanding directions, or misinterpreting the question (Chappuis, 2014; Fisher & Frey, 2010, 2015). Unlike misconceptions and reasoning errors, mistakes do not require significant instructional intervention unless the student is repeating the same mistake with consistency (for example, always failing to carefully read directions).

Misconceptions, if not caught early, can cause significant problems later in the learning. A misconception is more challenging to address because it is often based on a student's firsthand experience, observation of phenomena, or oversimplified interpretation of stated rules. Armed with pre-existing understanding, a student may have misconceptions based on a naïve perspective (for example, smaller things are always lighter in weight), a misunderstanding (for example, apostrophes show possession except when used in *it's*), or an inaccurate belief (for example, the sun rotates around the earth because it always rises in the east and sets in the west). Teachers might not easily spot misconceptions in the early phases of learning when checking simple answers, but misconceptions can reveal themselves later when students must integrate key concepts or solve problems.

On the other hand, students can make reasoning errors even when they understand the concepts. Reasoning, the process of thinking logically to form conclusions, judgments, arguments, inferences, or solutions from facts or concepts, can be fraught with errors, even when the concepts are accurate. Reasoning errors involve insufficiently or inaccurately applying a thinking skill to key concepts. Following are a few common reasoning errors.

- Misunderstanding the reasoning process
- Employing the reasoning process inaccurately or insufficiently
  - Unsupported claims
  - Insufficient evidence or sampling errors
  - Overgeneralizations or oversimplifications
  - Inconsistency (in evidence or application)
  - Omissions
  - Contradictions
  - Illogical thinking or non-sequitur errors

Students who demonstrate reasoning errors may have the concepts right but display limited skills when it comes to interpreting or manipulating those concepts in meaningful ways.

These inaccuracies pose problems for students who require targeted, precise instructional responses from teachers. All practice work requires feedback if teachers mean for practice to result in improvement.

## Homework

Sometimes, practice extends beyond the classroom, either to increase the quantity of practice or to capitalize on classroom time for instructional purposes. The raging debate about the value of homework and its potential impact on student learning has continued, it seems, throughout the history of formalized education (Gill &

Schlossman, 2004; Vatterott, 2009). Proponents believe that homework is a powerful instructional option (Canadian Council on Learning, 2009; Cooper, Robinson, & Patall, 2006; Marzano, 2007; Marzano & Pickering, 2007a, 2007b) that can increase student achievement, whereas opponents believe there is little value in homework (Bennett & Kalish, 2006; Kohn, 2006). Though some experts (Hattie, 2009; Vatterott, 2009) note that more precise research is required and there are unexplored variables that could certainly improve the effects of homework on learning, the argument has remained largely polarized with supporters on either end of the spectrum remaining fervent in their stance.

Research on *traditional* homework practice indicates that benefits are minimal and costs can be grave, especially when such a routine likely develops fixed mindsets in students and undermines their motivation to continue learning (Hattie, 2009). For example, the teacher assigns a set of practice items for students to complete at home, scores the assignment shortly afterward, enters results in the gradebook, and sometimes returns homework to students for use during test preparation. Hattie (2009) notes, "For these learners [struggling learners], homework can undermine motivation, internalize incorrect routines and strategies, and reinforce less effective study habits" (p. 235). In other words, when students generate marks, scores, or grades that provide no instructional insights for improvement (for example, a paper reveals a score of twelve correct out of twenty possible), they can feel hopeless and trapped. They interpret the negative—or even positive—scores to be a reflection of themselves and develop self-fulfilling beliefs and accompanying behaviors that block intellectual risk taking and future growth opportunities. Moreover, when students don't receive accurate or supportive feedback as they refine their knowledge and skills, they may continue to practice incorrectly and reinforce inaccurate routines or misconceptions. Repeating practice without quality feedback and informed interventions only serves to underscore a student's limitations.

Like all education research, the existing research on homework effectiveness is based on *what is currently happening* and not *what could be happening*. Vatterott (2009) notes that current research on homework is insufficient in both quantity and quality. More and better research is necessary, specifically focused on improved homework practices that serve as diagnostic tools to support instructional agility. Much like a superseded scientific theory (that is, one that a majority of experts no longer considers to be a viable description of reality or an accurate finding) that has been disproved in light of new evidence, homework as practice still offers the potential to provide an untapped reservoir of deep learning. In any field—sports, music, business, medicine, art, and so on—practice is the exclusive process that leads to excellence.

Undoubtedly, much would have to change in the traditional practice scenario if homework is to become a high-leverage strategy. Still, homework has yet to meet its full potential as an instructional practice that can generate invaluable information for teachers and students and ultimately, support and even inspire continued learning.

# Connections to Other Tenets

The work of practice, whether it occurs within a lesson or beyond the classroom, always boils down to giving students quality information that helps them improve over time. As such, practice connects to many of the assessment tenets, but the four most significant of these tenets are (1) purpose, (2) architecture, (3) communication, and (4) student investment.

Practice provides an assessment opportunity that is most often intended to be formative in nature. Practice provides students opportunities to take risks, make mistakes, refine their knowledge and skills, and track their own readiness and ability to certify their degrees of proficiency. It stands to reason that practice directly links to the purpose tenet. The processes teachers put in place must remain formative in nature in order to provide the scaffolding for a student's ultimate success. As such, teachers must use practice to increase hope, efficacy, and achievement.

Practice is a critical aspect of the tenet regarding assessment architecture. Teachers should never randomly assign homework following a lesson. They should invest much thought and care into selecting or designing practice opportunities, intentionally linking them to the learning targets at hand and providing meaningful insight into next steps for both students and themselves. Practice provides the scaffolded support that students need to be successful on the resulting summative assessment. The data and evidence students generate along the way should provide them with high degrees of confidence when they enter into the summative opportunities to prove what they have refined through their practice experiences.

The communication of homework results *must* generate a productive response for both students and teachers. For students, practice work should provide insights into personal strengths and opportunities to improve. Teachers should use practice work to gather feedback on student readiness and common misconceptions or errors, as well as to provide both success and intervention feedback so practice leads to improved performance on subsequent practice opportunities.

The most significant assessment tenet, however, is that of student investment. Teachers must use practice work to help students deeply invest in their own progress, supporting their ability to self-regulate and monitor achievement over time. In order for that to happen, teachers should offer practice work in a learning-rich culture that provides opportunities for risk taking, productive failure, and celebration of successes. Many changes in the traditional paradigm of practice are necessary if students are to maintain a sense of purpose, focus, growth over time, and personal pride in achievement.

# Practicing in Action

If practice is ever to really be about the opportunity to fail forward, then many things must change from the current paradigm of assign-score-record-return. Teachers must monitor all practice for learning—whether students perform it in a whole group, small groups, independently in class, or independently outside of class. Scoring for accuracy is not by itself a sufficient means of monitoring. Unmonitored practice misses the benefits and destroys hope for students along the way. In order to reap the full benefits of homework *as practice* and to use the emerging evidence required for instructional decision making, teachers and students must look at the evidence produced to determine if there are mistakes, misconceptions, or errors so they can gather the necessary feedback to practice better with each new effort.

The value of practice quickly unravels without attending to several cautionary notes. The context guidelines that must surround practice are as significant as the practice itself. Practice must be focused, manageable, and required; monitor mindsets and motivation; and foster responsibility and ownership of learning. These provide the backdrop of agreements to support the careful design of homework as well as the intentional interpretation of results.

## Focused Practice

Time is precious in the classroom; there's not a moment to waste. Therefore, all assigned practice must be intentional. In advance, teachers will want to develop practice opportunities that tie directly to the learning standards and targets and that likely reveal probable misconceptions or errors. And teachers will want to preplan their strategies for diagnosing the results of practice efforts so the entire class better understands learning expectations, and individual students better understand their strengths and opportunities for growth related to those expectations.

Teachers should first and foremost align focused practice to the standards and learning targets. Students always know precisely which learning target they are practicing. The learning targets are clear, and students are likely tracking their progress target by target within a single unit, giving them the opportunity to improve over time. All the evidence they generate from practice becomes fodder for class activities such as exploring examples of strong and weak work, clarifying criteria for quality, calibrating scoring to be consistent with teacher expectations, isolating common misconceptions and errors, identifying plausible instructional fixes, and providing students with targeted feedback that supports their independent instructional decision making.

Teachers need not assign homework daily. When students practice independently before a degree of readiness is in place, they can rehearse incorrectly and learn bad habits or solidify preexisting misconceptions, which can lead to frustration, confusion, and ultimately, time-intensive interventions to fix early errors. Instead, practice should only occur after students have a clear understanding of the expectations and the concepts they are working on.

Teachers can identify readiness during guided instruction. Fisher and Frey (2010) write, "Based on the responses to the question, the teacher uses probes, cues, and direct explanations in modeling and motivation to share the cognitive work with students" (p. 117). Classroom discussions that involve student-developed criteria for quality, collaborative scoring, diagnosing errors, and guided practice checks can produce evidence that helps teachers ensure students are ready to practice independently. So, teachers should not assign practice every day. Instead, they should intentionally assign it at key points to check whether each student has grasped the learning and can function independently.

## *Manageability*

More isn't always better. Why give twenty problems for students to practice if five robust tasks with a higher level of rigor provide more quality evidence of learning? In the case of practice, increased quantity does not lead to improved learning. In fact, one could make a strong case that fewer items requiring deeper analysis can improve the quality of the practice experience. A few well-designed items, prompts, or tasks provide sufficient opportunity for students to practice independently and ample time for teachers to engage students in meaningful diagnostics of the results. And a few robust items, prompts, or tasks can often shed more light into how a student understands the work as opposed to a long list of simple problems or rote responses marked right or wrong.

Hattie (2009) and Marzano (2007) both note that older students can handle more work; still, Marzano (2007) adds, there is a point at which too much homework negates the value of the practice and ultimately impedes learning. Fewer problems make practice manageable for students, provide better quality evidence for teachers, and allow teachers to diagnose problems robustly at the classroom level after students have completed their practice.

By its very nature, the act of grading work turns practice into a game in which the focus shifts to the results rather than the diagnostic opportunity to improve. If practice is to provide a safe zone for learning, then teachers should not incorporate early mistakes into the concluding, summative grade. In other words, teachers must provide students with penalty-free opportunities to explore mistakes, errors, and misconceptions while finding their way to accuracy in the required skills and concepts. When early failures eliminate opportunities for students to achieve mastery, then their hope, efficacy, and motivation decrease. Conversely, and equally demotivating, when early successes build a sufficient bank of points, then successful students can choose to opt out of caring about their own summative results, as they have already secured a good probability of passing. Homework requires feedback rather than evaluation marks or scores if it is to be successful in supporting continued learning for students.

## Required Versus Graded

Some educators are concerned that if they don't grade homework, students won't complete it. At some point, the terms *grading* and *requiring* seem to have become synonymous. The underlying premise is that if something is required, grading ensures that students will complete the task. Unfortunately, teachers are all too aware that the threat of a loss of points in the gradebook doesn't always guarantee that students complete homework; students neglecting their homework is a timeless phenomenon.

There are other ways to require that students complete work. For example, teachers could make completed work and the resulting feedback into gateways to next steps in the learning journey, which students must submit or complete to advance to the next level and learn more. There are two significant ways to entice students to complete homework. First, make the resulting feedback invaluable to students' future success. Second, empower students to use their results from the homework experience to make informed instructional decisions about what comes next in their learning.

This means when students do not do the work, the consequence they face is to do the work right when they walk into class (no loss of points). While others engage in some kind of activity that involves using the homework, those who have not completed the homework are doing it. This provides the teacher an opportunity to understand whether the incomplete work was about students not knowing what to do or some other reason. New systems of shared responsibility (such as data tracking, peer and self-evaluation, and goal setting) are required at the classroom level in order for teachers to stop evaluating homework with traditional marks, scores, or grades.

## Responsibility

Using grades to reward or punish never actually teaches responsibility. If anything, the decision to accept the punishment allows students to opt out of learning responsibility. When teachers use grades as punishment or reward systems, they miss the mark of their primary purpose—to certify mastery against a given standard.

Vatterott (2009) writes:

> *Responsibility* is often a code word for *obedience.* When we say we want students to be *responsible,* are we saying we want them to be *obedient*— to do *what* we want them to do *when* we want them to do it, to be mind- less drones, blindly obedient to authority? (p. 11)

Vatterott (2009) notes that there are more powerful ways to teach responsibility, "involving [students] in decision making about their learning, teaching them how to self-assess, letting them design learning tasks, or allowing them to help manage classroom and school facilities" (p. 11). Teachers must give students true responsi- bility, which involves their ability to make decisions and accept the consequences of those decisions, that is, consequences that are natural to the situation (like missing key feedback to improve or missing opportunities to advance) and not contrived (like missing points and reducing grades).

## Ownership

Learning is an extremely social activity, and teachers must establish structures to leverage the power of such significant learning opportunities. However, when it comes to verifying what an individual student knows, can do, needs to know, or struggles to do, looking at unreliable data does not help. When students complete practice work beyond the teacher's purview or within a collaborative setting, teach- ers have no guarantee that the resulting evidence is in fact the intellectual work of the student who submits it. It works best when teachers use prompts, cues, and homework checks that require students to produce independent samples while under observation. In the end, it is just as inappropriate to award students points for inau- thentic work as it is to make instructional decisions for students based on inaccurate or insufficient evidence.

## Mindsets and Motivation

Practice must provide safe opportunities for students to take intellectual risks. It's important, then, to monitor the motivation levels and mindsets of students who engage in practice work. Are they committed to improving? Are they tracking their progress? Are they asserting their own learning needs? The evidence teachers generate when answering these questions determines whether or not the practice systems and guidelines they have implemented are effective. As it turns out, mindsets are as sus- ceptible to becoming entrenched and erroneous as content knowledge and skill-based habits. It's incredibly challenging to relearn something anew. It is even more challeng- ing to change a fixed mindset. Practice can be powerful *if* navigated with feedback to correct misconceptions, mistakes, and errors before they become engrained.

In sum, practice matters. Practicing "sharpens the saw" to effect change and guarantee success. But the guidelines outlined here are not necessarily the norm in traditional classrooms. Teachers must employ new strategies and actions in order for practice to begin to matter to the students.

# Strategies and Tools

The following strategies can help teachers begin to change the culture around practice in classrooms. They provide a structure teachers may explore to engage students in a new way of thinking about homework and practice. The overall goal is to make practice more meaningful and achievement more possible.

## Strategy 1: Employ Practice Checks

Practice checks are an important strategy for identifying what each student knows and can do. When practice happens in a group or beyond the purview of the teacher via homework, the teacher cannot draw an accurate conclusion or make an informed instructional decision. It's entirely possible that students had help completing the task from peers or parents and that they themselves might not yet understand how to accomplish the task independently.

During a practice check, a teacher asks students to reproduce a sample of the practice work independently and on demand. For example, the teacher might ask students to set aside their homework or their in-class group work so they cannot see it. Then, students reproduce the answer to, for example, the third homework item individually on a clean piece of paper within an abbreviated time frame. Or, the teacher might provide students with an item that is similar but not exactly the same as a homework item to complete as a check for understanding.

As an alternative, teachers ask students to solve one or two problems, such as those studied during class time, on an exit ticket. Students hand in the exit ticket to the teacher as they leave for the day. Teachers use the exit tickets, with or without student names on them, to identify the quantity and types of errors students are making. This process gives teachers reflection time and allows them to make decisions for follow-up instruction the next day.

Teachers should not require practice checks every day; in fact, they should be sporadic enough that students won't always be able to predict when a practice check is about to occur. While homework and group practice are important and essential to learning, this work should never go into the gradebook to help determine proficiency in student learning. Teachers should use practice checks to note areas of strength and areas needing improvement as part of the formative data to inform them how to move forward with instruction.

As an added benefit, practice checks can stop the madness of chasing students to complete homework. If students previously practiced by doing homework, they will likely find the practice check to be relatively easy. However, if students did not practice by doing homework, they still have the opportunity to prove what they can do. The evidence is far more reliable, and the practice provides students with the opportunity to make strategic decisions about where best to concentrate their efforts.

When teachers employ this strategy, the resulting data provide more accurate information about what individual students know and can do. Moreover, students begin to understand the benefit of rehearsing in advance for something they may see in the immediate future.

## Strategy 2: Highlight and Analyze Errors

The reflective conversation that follows practice must provide meaningful feedback. One strategy that teachers can use involves going on an error hunt to isolate common errors. Once they find errors, the whole class, student groups, or partners can diagnose the type of errors made and generate plausible strategies they can use to avoid making the same errors in the future. As we outline in table 6.1, there are many ways to accomplish this task.

*Table 6.1: Options for Analyzing Errors*

| Option | Group Size | Sample Size | When Appropriate | Strategy |
|--------|-----------|-------------|------------------|----------|
| 1 | Whole class | One | Following an in-class team effort or a practice check | Skim through the samples provided and select one that best demonstrates a type of common error. |
| | | | | Illustrate the error by typing or rewriting it so students' handwriting is not revealed. |
| | | | | Engage the class in isolating where the error took place. Once you identify the error, engage students in analyzing the type of error and generating plans for how to avoid that error in the future. |
| | | | | Use an anchor chart to keep track of the types of errors students commonly make with each particular skill or concept. |

continued ➜

| Option | Group Size | Sample Size | When Appropriate | Strategy |
|---|---|---|---|---|
| 2 | Small teams | Many | Following the use of an exit ticket or a formal assessment | Gather a set of samples from a different classroom. The samples should not have names on them. Teachers should preview the samples in advance in order to guarantee quality examples are provided. |
| | | | | Place students in groups and provide them with note cards from an exit ticket or strips of paper that contain a specific copied item from a formal assessment. |
| | | | | Engage students in placing samples into piles of strong and weak work. Then have them divide the piles based on the types of errors. |
| | | | | Ask groups to compare notes regarding their findings and document them using an anchor chart or similar tool. |
| 3 | Whole class or small teams | One to four or five | Following a single-item assessment such as an exit ticket or practice check scored on a rubric | Skim through the samples provided and select a sample for each level of the rubric that best demonstrates a type of common error. |
| | | | | Type or rewrite the sample so no student's name or handwriting is revealed. Project each selected sample (one at a time), and engage the entire class or small groups of students in collaboratively scoring the work, isolating the errors, and defending their responses with evidence. |
| 4 | Small teams | One sample per student | Immediately following homework | Ask students to remove their homework from the previous evening for analysis. |
| | | | | Show the correct answers on the board and have students highlight or check off any incorrect items. |
| | | | | Engage a small team in analyzing the types of errors and identifying the instructional fix for each type. |
| | | | | Have students document their own common types of errors and establish a goal to remove such areas from future work. |

| 5 | Self-editing | One per person | Prior to submitting practice work | Ask students to highlight any errors they think they might have made before submitting their work. |
|---|---|---|---|---|
| | | | | Use a different colored highlighter to highlight the errors you find. |
| | | | | Return to work. Engage students in analyzing the errors you both identified as well as those only one of you identified. |
| | | | | Have students name and fix the errors you identified. Have them clarify the errors you disagreed about. |

No matter how teachers decide to isolate and analyze errors, it is imperative that students feel safe in the process. Teachers should never reveal a student's name or handwriting during large-group discussion. It is inevitable that students will see each other's work during peer-to-peer activities, and even that must occur within guidelines that teachers establish with the entire class in order to understand how to respond to errors with the appropriate finesse.

Teaching students how to analyze errors can accomplish three significant, long-term benefits: teachers exponentially increase (1) the quantity of feedback students receive because now they are getting a steady dose of it, (2) the quality of feedback students receive because it is calibrated and consistent with teacher feedback, and (3) students' capacity to close the learning gap because they can see what they need to fix and know how to fix it.

## Strategy 3: Track Student Readiness and Celebrate Success

Tracking student errors can be a powerful activity, and creating anchor charts can help students recognize errors more quickly and analyze them more accurately. But tracking errors is only one part of the equation. It is equally important for students to acknowledge and celebrate successes.

One strategy teachers can use involves tracking the class average on readiness for the summative assessment target by target and skill by skill. When students can see, for example, that 78 percent of the class has mastered target 2, they enter the summative phases of learning with an increased level of confidence and collective efficacy. Moreover, students tend to work more collaboratively to ensure they are all ready for summative assessment. Placing success charts next to anchor charts that document errors by learning target helps students actually *see* the progress they are making.

Celebrating success not only emphasizes *what's right* but also highlights *what's valued*. What gets celebrated gets replicated.

When striving to create internal motivation, a critical component of student investment, celebration should not come in the form of praise, parties, or extrinsic rewards. In fact, there are a few things to know about celebrating learning. First, the celebrated people, events, or accomplishments should meet the following criteria. They should:

- Offer a genuine or worthy cause for celebration (not trite or oversimplified)

- Rest on trustworthy (reliable and accurate) evidence of achievement

- Align with that which the teacher is striving to foster, support, or develop

- Serve as a model that students can and should replicate

Teachers should exclusively use public celebrations of learning for whole-class success. When they publicly celebrate individual students, the process generates a visible divide between the haves and have nots, breaking the culture of learning and reducing the probability that students will feel safe taking future risks.

Second, the teacher must also attend to his or her own efforts with care. The *how* behind a teacher's celebratory words is as significant as the words themselves. It's important that teachers strive to address all of the following when celebrating learning in their classrooms.

- Be authentic and sincere.

- Be informed of key details such as hurdles, problems, successes, and characteristics.

- Stick to the impressive *learning-centered* facts and avoid general *learner-focused* praise.

- Emphasize the value of learning in a broader context (for example, avoid feedback that focuses on how pleased you are).

- Highlight specifics worth replicating and keep the focus appropriately on point.

Surprisingly, students of all ages respond better to celebrations that meet all of these criteria than they do to parties, extrinsic rewards, or gushy feedback about how great they are. Well-timed, authentic insights can inspire intrinsic motivation (Ryan & Deci, 2000).

# Strategy 4: Have Students Self-Monitor

Like the classwide data charts to track success, students will benefit from tracking their own progress over time. Student reflection following a learning experience can lead to personal understanding regarding what worked and what didn't; stringing such events together over time allows students to see patterns in the emerging data that can provide empowering information. Ultimately, students must be the decision makers regarding their progress while learning. It is helpful when students record the results of their performance over time in data notebooks, learning journals, or personal portfolios. No matter the medium, students need to see a visible trajectory of growth. Data tracking with data tools is a required feature within the option the teacher selects for recording evidence.

Simply recording the data will not suffice. Teachers must follow certain guidelines if the data are to support continued learning and the recording process is to provide resources that increase motivation and growth. For example:

- Learning goals must be tied to learning standards.

- Data should not be perceptual (for example, self-assessment scores like, "I think I'm a 3") when used to make decisions. All tracked data must be evidence based.

- Data sheets must be few and meaningful. When everything is a goal, then there really are no goals. Learners must track the *essentials*.

- Data that are tracked must show progress between assessments. This extends far beyond simply documenting pre and post data and includes incremental improvements between the pre/post assessments.

- Data must be organized in visual ways—bar graphs, pie graphs, run charts, etc.—so that the learner can see progress being made.

- The learners must be in their data notebooks regularly. This might not mean daily, but it does mean *often enough to inspire action between assessments*.

- The learners must be the ones making the additions and notations in their books because it's *their* data. When teachers record the data for them, the data have minimal impact on the learner's motivation or growth mindset. It does not matter if learners fill in their check boxes or bar graphs in sloppy ways so the notebooks are not pretty for parents. It matters that the data are *owned* by the primary stakeholder and that same stakeholder can then make better decisions as a result.

- Data must be confidential. No child should ever be revealed for his/her results in the data notebooks or on the data walls in the classrooms and hallways.
- Effective formative feedback and reflection strategies are necessary to engage learners meaningfully as they interact with their data while on the learning journey. (Erkens, 2013)

Tracking through the use of data notebooks allows teachers to respond in the moment and over time to students' progress. Students benefit by learning how to reflect on and track their progress. When students see progress in a visual way and over time, they gain confidence, which helps them persist and become more motivated (Hattie & Timperley, 2007). This connects the idea of practice with mobilizing—these are both essential actions and outcomes of quality instructional agility practice. When teachers choose to use data notebooks in the classroom, they must do so with great care and remember the Hippocratic Oath, which can apply just as well to education as it does to medicine: "Above all, do no harm." Using data to label, sort, or highlight incompetence violates the very core of the Hippocratic Oath. Teachers must maintain respect for students and the learning process.

## Strategy 5: Conduct Brief, Sporadic Learning Conferences

While data gathering and student self-monitoring are incredibly powerful, they're not sufficient without teacher involvement in the process. Fisher and Frey (2010) write, "Guided instruction, at its heart, is a dialogue between teacher and learner. However, at times the teacher must reassume cognitive responsibility and temporarily take it away from the learner in order to provide a direct explanation" (p. 98).

More compelling and influential than giving and recording grades, teachers can give short and focused bursts of personal feedback while simultaneously employing their own professional judgment to continually monitor each student's progress. When monitoring learning, it is important that teachers constantly circulate around the room and ask students to reference their personal data in order to supply evidence of learning and validate their understanding. What's on paper may be impressive, but students must prove it true with spot checks that require them to solve a new problem or explain their thinking in an existing example.

Teachers should integrate learning interviews into the general practice of moving about the classroom. They can conduct these interviews in less than a minute in a relatively private manner. Teachers might use interviews to check for understanding, and students can use them to seek permission to customize their learning journey with data and artifacts. A simple formula for a one-minute learning interview would include the following steps.

- The initiator (teacher or student) establishes the purpose for the interview (two seconds).

- Clarify the learning target to anchor the conversation (five seconds).

- Examine the existing data and artifacts (fifteen seconds).

- Offer a prompt for validation (thirty seconds).

  - Provide a new problem for the student to solve. (Note: If the problem will take more time to solve than the allotted thirty seconds, walk away from the student until he or she completes the task and reconvene to finish the interview when the student is ready.)

  - Select an existing artifact (for example, question 5 on last night's homework), and ask the student to explain the thinking, errors, or celebration behind the work. (Note: Let the student decide if the work is right or wrong.)

- Provide quick feedback that highlights next steps based on the results of the validation task (seven seconds).

Another powerful strategy to use during practice review is to mark a few items on a student's paper, intentionally selecting some that are accurate and some that are not. Then require the student to double-check his or her answer to these items to validate the thinking process.

One-minute interviews are quick and easy. They are necessary if teachers want to keep a hands-on approach to monitoring the evidence students record in the data notebook. A more comprehensive conversation can happen in what Chappuis (2014) calls the three-minute conference. Three-minute conferences are more formal in that they involve advanced preparation. The student must analyze his or her work and come to the conference prepared to identify personal strengths and opportunities to grow. He or she is responsible for recording notes from the conference. Chappuis (2014) writes that each minute of the three-minute conference serves a specific purpose, and the student must be the primary recorder of all findings, including teacher feedback.

- **Minute 1:** The student outlines strengths and opportunities for growth while referencing his or her work.

- **Minute 2:** The teacher adds feedback regarding his or her view of the student's strengths and opportunities for growth while referencing the student's work. The student records the teacher's ideas.

- **Minute 3:** Together, the teacher and student agree on next steps. The student continues to record the agreements in writing.

Focused learning conversations, such as the one-minute interview or the three-minute conference, are necessary so the teacher remains the key point of reference regarding students' progress over time. The diagnostics of what is going wrong can directly inform a targeted response from instructional decision makers—both the teacher and the students. Fisher and Frey (2007) note, "When their teachers regularly check for understanding, students become increasingly aware of how to monitor their own understanding" (p. 3).

## Strategy 6: Focus and Customize Practice

*Source: Adapted from Erkens, 2014.*

If homework is to serve as formative data, then it needs to be *instructionally sensitive* for both student and teacher alike. Ideally, then, what happened with homework the night before should inform a classroom teacher's instruction immediately the next day. Rather than simply correcting right and wrong answers and then collecting the homework papers to be recorded somewhere, teachers must consider meaningful and interactive ways to create engaging learning conversations and generate quality, supportive information for the *next* lesson following the completion of the practice experience.

Imagine, for example, that a teacher created varying options for homework like the following.

> On tonight's homework, there are three learning targets. You must answer a minimum of three questions per target area, but (1) if you have tried the questions but are struggling, then don't answer any more questions in that section—instead, write out your questions or misunderstandings regarding that target and come prepared to talk about what you don't understand; (2) if you answered all of the questions in that target area but are unsure you have right answers, then self-assign and try a few more on your own to see if you can figure it out; or (3) if you are certain that you have mastered the question in that target area, then please write two or three test questions that you think I could use to assess that target. If your questions are good ones, they may show up on our next test.

Clearly, when the learners enter the room the next day there will be a variety of things happening in the homework assignment, and simply marking right or wrong answers will not be helpful.

The teacher seeks to generate *formative data* for *instructionally sensitive responses* by using a variety of strategies. It might play out like this.

All right, everyone, let's take out last night's homework and begin our learning for today.

- **Target 1: Dots and Error Analysis**—Remember, target 1 included questions 1 through 5. This was review for us as we've already done a lot of work with target 1. The correct answers are provided on the board. Put a dot next to any answer you have that is wrong. Now, get into small groups and analyze each other's dots. See if you can identify the *type* of error that was made. Name the error and help your peers identify the strategies needed to fix that type of error. If you had any questions or concerns about this section, you can skip the error analysis work and meet with me by the back table so I can better understand your concerns.

- **Target 2: Four Corners**—Let's move on to target 2. Target 2 included questions 6–12, and we haven't done as much work with this target yet. Let's take a look at question 10 because it's a really good example of this target area. If you answered question 10 like this (answer revealed), please stand in the corner marked with books. If you answered like this (answer revealed), please stand in the corner by my desk. If you answered like this (answer revealed), please stand in the corner by the door. If you didn't know the answer, it's okay because we're still learning this target. Please stand in the corner by the windows.

  Now, wherever you are standing, you must talk with your peers as to why you have that answer and if you are the corner that didn't know the answer, I want you to discuss what was hard about that question. You can move to any new corner at any time, but if you move, you must be prepared to explain your decision. (Note: In this activity, the teacher has immediate visible data as to who understands and who does not. The teacher stands in the middle of the room to hear discussions and identify misconceptions [two of the corners] or misunderstandings or confusion [corner with no answers]. After about two minutes, the teacher calls for a large-group discussion to highlight the right answer and discuss the popular types of errors that can be made with the target area as well as the possible strategies needed to address the errors.)

- **Target 3: Student-Generated Responses**—Target 3 included questions 13–20. It was brand new yesterday, and I anticipate there may have been a lot of questions or concerns. Did anyone have any questions

continued ➤

> or concerns about this target area? (*Teacher notes all questions and concerns on the board.*) Did anyone have any possible test questions that you generated last night that you might be willing to share right now? (*Teacher asks a few of the learners to write a question on the board.*) Great. Let's use this question (points to option) to answer this concern (*points to concern*). Let's work it out as a group. (All answers are discussed in lieu of what was not understood as a means to build deeper understanding.)
>
> Okay, everyone, take a minute to reflect on your work last night by looking at all three target areas and note where you will need to be spending more time and practice as we continue our learning together.

Even though reviewing homework in this manner continues the teaching process, some teachers might not feel they have the luxury of time to go to such depth. If so, two time-saving options follow.

1.  Identify one or two questions that are similar to the homework problems (but not exactly the same) and have students fill them out immediately upon entering the classroom. They can even reference last night's homework if they have it done. Once students have answers on their slip, they can partner with one to two others to compare answers (individuals can still change answers at this point), discuss how they arrived at the answers they have, and develop a rationale statement for why they think their answers are correct. Identify a few teams to share their answer to question 1 and get feedback and corrections from *other* teams in the room before giving the actual answer. Then move to the next question using the same process.

2.  Identify one question that captures the essence of last night's homework and engage the learners in a large-group error analysis activity, highlighting common errors and recording the type of error and its companion fix on an anchor chart.

In the end, homework that is intended to provide learners with practice opportunities requires that learners engage in safe opportunities to discuss successes and mistakes and receive clear, specific feedback that will help them improve. If the homework is not graded and the conversations are aimed solely at supporting all learners in mastering the targets at hand, then the feedback practices are low risk and a true culture of *learning* can be built. Such practices highlight formative assessment at its best because the teacher has activated the learners as resources to one another as well as instructional decision makers regarding their own learning needs. Homework can provide powerful formative data when it engages teachers and learners in deep discussion and becomes a tool for *continuing the learning* the next day. *Formative assessment and quality teaching* are two sides of the same coin.

# Conclusion

John Wooden is recognized as one of the finest coaches in history, and the secret to his success was reportedly his dogged focus on practice. Doug Lemov et al. (2012) explain:

> He kept a record of every practice on note cards, which he filed away for future reference: what worked; what didn't; how to do it better next time. Unlike many coaches, he focused not on scrimmaging—playing in a way that *replicated* the game—but on drilling, that is playing in ways that intentionally *distorted* the game to emphasize and isolate specific concepts and skills. He followed a logical progression, often starting his instruction on topics like shooting by having players work without the ball and building to increasingly challenging applications. He repeated drills until his players achieved mastery and then automaticity, even if it meant not drilling on more sophisticated topics . . . . And he always insisted that his players practice doing it—whatever "it" was—right. (p. xx)

In order to support agility, teachers must interpret evidence as it emerges during the instructional phases. Practice provides rich opportunities to gather evidence that teachers and students can use to check for understanding and move forward. It must focus on continual improvement, and students must have the opportunity to succeed at high levels, even though they made mistakes during practice opportunities. As Heath notes, "To practice isn't to declare, *I'm bad*. To practice it is to declare, *I can be better*" (as cited in Lemov et al., 2012, p. 11).

# Pause and Ponder

Take a few moments to reflect on the following questions.

- What role does practice play in helping learners achieve at high levels? Describe the two conditions necessary to make practice a powerful learning tool.

- What role does feedback play in making practice meaningful for students?

- What does the research say about homework? How does this influence your current policies and practices?

- How could we create structures that entice students to do homework—to practice?

- Of the six strategies that enhance the practice in which students engage, which are familiar? Which provide a new way of thinking about practice? Which have potential to help students learn at higher levels?

# CHAPTER 7
# VIEWING INSTRUCTIONAL AGILITY IN THE BROADER CONTEXT

*In systems thinking, the true wisdom often comes from a willingness to let go of past learning.*

—Pearl Zhu

Agility means graceful, nimble, flexible, responsive, and quick. Any one of these words describes the state of being or action taken when an individual, team, school, or system is agile. The broader context, including the larger district, jurisdiction, and school, influences the culture in which students and teachers thrive. This chapter addresses how the broader context establishes the conditions for instructional agility to take hold.

A *graceful* system communicates its expectations and builds on the strengths of individuals and teams within it. District and school leaders, along with others working with and for teachers, should commit to a tone of possibility. Their words and actions need to reflect a vision focused on learning. The more confident teachers feel, the more potential for them to develop a positive tone in the classroom that supports students achieving at high levels. The more teachers feel heard, the more confident and invested they become in the system. For example, we can see graceful agility when people perhaps resist a bit, but the system and individuals seek to understand that resistance and provide the support necessary to engage in meaningful assessment work. Grace creates trust and a sense of efficacy. When teachers feel like those in the system believe in their capacity to do amazing work with learners, there is a sense of optimism and confidence. That positively influences the daily interactions teachers have with students.

The opposite of that is when the system meets resistance with more policies that punish rather than support. For example, perhaps there is a sense that some collaborative teams are not doing the work intended. Instead of training those teams or supporting those teams in direct ways to guide and help develop that practice, a punitive policy asks teachers to submit agendas or assessments or something else that doesn't help solve the problem. A graceful system has its eye on the vision and, with clear expectations, responds with flexible and differentiated support.

Being *nimble* in the broader context means the system (for example, the school, jurisdiction, and district) acknowledges that there are contextual differences within and among grade levels, courses, teachers, and disciplines. As a result, the vision remains a common vision for the entire system, but how it plays out is again *flexible* and *responsive*. Art, music, and physical education are performance based; kindergarteners and first graders learn at different rates; observation and feedback look different in these two contexts; and mapping out the learning for these grade levels and disciplines is different. Nimble systems embrace these differences and are flexible and responsive because they allow different disciplines to respond. A nimble system helps teachers feel empowered and gain confidence in providing the best possible experience and conditions for students to engage deeply and achieve at high levels. Teachers must feel they can flex and respond with the end goal being higher achievement and confidence for students. A nimble system gains power and moves in rhythm with those differences.

Being *quick* and timely means that how the educators accomplish the work is flexible. It doesn't take a committee meeting to move forward when the work's larger vision is in place. It means getting clear about learning and sharing that with students. A system must have a clear vision that allows for flexibility and responsiveness when it matters most. When teachers engage in deep planning and design, they come to understand what it means to work in the moment. It is critical that teachers feel empowered to make those decisions in the moment without the system providing too many barriers. Being agile means a system's response is timely, or quick—aligned with a vision and a framework of what it wants, but not rigid in implementation. This work looks different in kindergarten than it does in calculus. As a result, the system must be able to set policies and expectations, hold schools and teachers to high expectations, yet allow for flexibility so that student learning can be the measure of success.

Let us illustrate a good example of instructional agility at a school level. Teachers meet professional learning days with great excitement or great dread, depending on many factors. In 2016, at a high school in northern Minnesota, principal Shane Zutz, in partnership with curriculum director Sara Olson, created a culture of high expectations, trust, and learning. When looking at student achievement, they knew they needed to make some adjustments. They began their journey to create a positive, rich culture in the school where teachers feel empowered and students learn at high levels. Their journey included (among other commitments to building a positive culture) engaging teachers in identifying essential standards or learning for each course, teasing out learning targets, and sharing those learning targets with students.

As they moved deeper into assessment design, they provided staff with some training on assessment design during an August learning day. After surveying each department and assessing where it was in its implementation of this work, Shane met with each department head and co-constructed an agenda for each group for their upcoming professional learning day in October of 2016. The agendas included questions and emerging issues specific to the department.

The whole group of teachers met in the morning for thirty minutes to talk about how to select an assessment method and then again in the afternoon for each department to share its progress. Throughout the day, the administrators touched base with each department to address concerns and challenges and support their learning work.

This is a strong example of a principal and curriculum director demonstrating instructional agility. Teachers left feeling more confident and excited about the work they were doing. The vision and outcomes were the same (clearly aligned standards to courses and assessments for the purpose of helping students achieve at higher levels), but the work was flexible and focused on the needs of each group. A system that does this has created a broader context of agility.

# The Main Idea

We can find instructionally agile teachers everywhere—they respond and pivot when they recognize and interpret students' misconceptions or understanding to push students to their next level of learning. However, to help inspire and move all teachers to a more intentional practice, we must establish predictable routines and habits at the school and district level. Ideally, teachers are compelled to respond and see the possibility to help all students achieve at high levels, despite the varied needs and backgrounds of students who walk through their doors. This type of intentional agility requires a *system*, a *culture*, and attention to the *broader context* to empower teachers to work collaboratively and independently. Teachers, ideally in teams, do the following.

- Develop a clear learning progression for students, both horizontally and vertically (assessment architecture)

- Design and choose student work and assessment artifacts that provide feedback and evidence of proficiency levels (assessment architecture, purpose, and communication)

- Employ a targeted response to push all students to achieve essential standards and beyond (instructional agility and student investment)

A system will help schools, teams, and teachers understand these concepts and then provide routines and resources to ensure their implementation. That supportive system intentionally seeks to know how its teachers understand their role of teaching and learning. In the introduction to *Blended: Using Disruptive Innovation to Improve Schools*, Clayton M. Christensen reflects on the changing demands on schools and the context in which educators live and work:

> I have been a good teacher for students who thought as I did or had experiences like mine. I am mediocre, at best, in teaching students who frame the world differently. . . . To have intellectually stimulating discussions with my students, I had to keep enrollment down. I always thought the teacher taught and the students listened. No longer. Stimulating discussions among large numbers of students in widely differing locations is now possible. Students can teach one another in addition to teachers teaching students. We are all learning how to learn and teaching how to teach. And thank goodness. As Eric Hoffer remarked, "In a time of drastic change it is the students who inherit the future. The learned usually find themselves beautifully equipped to live in a world that no longer exists." (as cited in Horn & Staker, 2015, p. xx)

This reflects the changing mindset that occurs as educators embrace the power of becoming instructionally agile. Students experience change at greater levels than ever before. Educators, in their efforts to guide and educate students to be productive citizens, must create the conditions in which students learn how to navigate these changes. So, the system must develop and support teachers in nurturing all people as students *and* teachers. Our changing society requires citizens who know how to learn because what may be true today may or may not be true tomorrow. There is much more of a demand to understand how to critique ideas, put different ideas together to solve problems, and prioritize how to move forward in a world that is increasingly fast paced and connected (connected to those crosscurricular competencies that we describe in chapter 5). Responding to students and pushing their learning to the next level are central to creating schools and classrooms where they invest in their learning.

In the broader context, schools and districts must be agile and responsive to the fluid demands students have in their efforts to thrive and contribute in the larger society. This means that the system must also help teachers fill this new role. This might mean changing the way we assess, a day's structure, and the assessment practices needed to make this possible. As new and innovative ways of helping students learn at high levels emerge, the system must respond and support teachers, teams, and students to meet these changing demands.

# Connections to Other Tenets

Instructional agility connects to all five of the other essential assessment tenets, but two in particular are important to supporting instructional agility. We describe assessment architecture and accurate interpretation here and with accompanying questions to guide instructional agility development at the system level.

- **Assessment architecture:** Plan the learning, design and choose evidence to show mastery, and prioritize the learning that all students must achieve. Be precise in what educators want their students to learn and how they progress.

  - How do teachers describe what they want their students to learn? Do teachers have learning progressions that map out their assessment architecture?

  - Can students describe what they are learning and where they are in their learning?

  - Are teachers clear about which evidence provides information for each standard?

  - Can students describe what their assessment evidence means in terms of their learning?

  - When students do or don't learn, do they get enrichment and is additional time built in for students to learn the prioritized standards?

- **Accurate interpretation:** Teacher teams work together to discuss what standards and learning mean in terms of student work; to review and calibrate their scoring of that work; and to come to consensus on what they think the work means in terms of strengths and misconceptions or next steps to grow. When the system has accurate, reliable evidence that reveals a program or practice isn't working, it is flexible enough to change and revise its response. Those closest to the implementation embrace this response, as they have been part of assessing the impact on students' achievement and confidence. When teams review assessment evidence and realize that students don't understand something, they intentionally build in instructional time.

- Is there a designated time when teachers meet to collaborate and talk about learning?

- Is there time and support for teachers meeting to examine student work and look at assessment evidence to determine what students know and how they can grow or take their next step in learning?

Assessment architecture and accurate interpretation are key aspects of instructional agility. A commitment to develop a culture of learning surrounds all the tenets. A system creates this culture of learning through a few key commitments that foster confidence and achievement. The next section describes these commitments and ways of being.

# Commitments to Fostering Instructional Agility

Confident and excited teachers make confident and excited students. Jim Knight (2007), an expert on instructional coaching, suggests, "When people talk about learning, the experience should be exciting, energizing, and empowering" (p. ix). Assessment has the potential to generate all of these conditions when teachers design and use it in the service of learning. It is a place's culture, the ways people there exist and interact, that often creates the space and inspiration to thrive. Culture often is enacted with four key commitments.

1. Believe in those with whom you work.
2. Provide ample time to think and innovate.
3. Co-design learning with students (in classrooms) and teachers (for their professional learning).
4. Use feedback to increase confidence and achievement.

## Commitment 1: Believe in Those With Whom You Work

The following describes the commitments that drive practices and policies in learning-centered organizations: "Believe in the capacity of those with whom the system works and signal this belief through providing ample time to grapple and apply import-ant ideas. Trust others" (Horn & Staker, 2015, p. xx). Teachers need to commit to believing in each other and trusting that everyone is doing the absolute best he or she can. When this trust exists, teachers are more willing to take risks and try innovative practices. As a result, teachers and teams need space to think. That means refraining from scheduling every minute of collaborative time and instead providing the vision and practice and allowing teachers to work the process.

## Commitment 2: Provide Ample Time to Think and Innovate

Margaret Heritage, a leading researcher in the field of classroom assessment, made a passionate plea to a group of educators attending a symposium at the 2016 American Educational Research Association annual meeting in Washington, D.C. She noted that to increase the capacity of teachers, leaders must provide them "the intellectual space to think" (Charteris & Smardon, 2015, p. 121, as cited in Willis & Adie, 2016, p. 10). When educators focus their efforts and protect ample amounts of time for reflection and application, they see results. This act fosters a sense of efficacy, signaling that leaders believe their teachers have the capacity to do amazing work that impacts student achievement and confidence.

## Commitment 3: Co-Design Learning With Students and Teachers

Co-design can happen when constructing quality criteria together. As teachers and students examine strong and weak work samples, they can co-construct a list of criteria. With this list and the work samples, a clearer picture of what quality learning looks like and a clearer vision of expectations take root. This leads to higher-quality work. The co-design process works beautifully to empower teachers. As schools and districts aim to improve the quality of their assessment practices, why not ask teachers to co-design the process and the products that help assessment create this culture of learning? Through the co-design process, a sense of pride and confidence emerges as students struggle and then land on something they are excited about, which leads to a sense of ownership and investment (Ruiz-Primo & Li, 2013). This investment is also true for teachers when they co-design their own learning.

## Commitment 4: Use Feedback to Increase Confidence and Achievement

When feedback is a regular practice and those in the system get used to giving, receiving, and acting on it, educators can create a culture of learning and growing. Feedback for the sake of growth and improvement is very different from evaluation. Often when teachers accompany feedback with numbers, the feedback feels evaluative. The best feedback describes evidenced strengths so the receiver can understand how to maintain good work and then provides a question or a step forward. None of those descriptions requires a number. In fact, the number can be distracting.

The following story sets the stage for how effective feedback can promote investment and a culture where people want to learn. Nicole sat next to a man from Alberta on an early morning flight. While she was ready to sleep, Jay was ready to talk. Jay was a software developer by day and artist by night. He claimed he could teach Nicole to draw in the time it took to fly from Oklahoma City to Minneapolis. She agreed to the challenge, and he was right.

He divided a piece of paper into four equal sections and pulled out a picture of a tiger. Jay told Nicole to draw it. He told her he would provide targeted feedback during the experiment, which would last only a short thirty minutes. For her first drawing, she had seven minutes. Then he gave her some feedback and a strategy for looking at proportions. After seven minutes, Nicole had little drawn, but had improved the proportions. In the final seven minutes, she was to get more of the shape and shading in place. Her third drawing was dramatically better than the first and second. It was engaging to get that targeted feedback and use it immediately. Seeing growth and improvement from the feedback was empowering. Drawing again and again helped Nicole improve and lessened her worry about getting it right immediately. This worry can undermine confidence and delay the practice that guides improvement. It was only thirty minutes, but she was pretty excited about her drawings, as shown in figure 7.1.

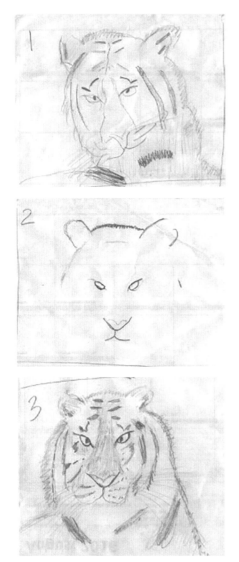

*Figure 7.1: Tiger drawings.*

Providing feedback—both strengths and next steps—and ample time to revise creates a culture where learning is a process and feedback is expected. As teachers implement new strategies for instructional agility, what kind of feedback do they receive and what kind of reflection do they do? When this feedback and reflection lead to developing the new strategies to be more effective, we create a culture of learning.

Feedback that leads to growth can have the same effect on students. It is this growth that helps students persist through challenging moments. What if students took one sentence or one paragraph and wrote it, got some feedback, rewrote it, got some more feedback, and rewrote it again? What if students got a mathematics problem and solved it, got some feedback, and then solved it again and again? How would this type of practice help build confidence and achievement? Granted, teachers can't do this all the time, but they could focus on one or two of the important skills, and that confidence and excitement will be contagious.

And, how does the concept of engaging students in feedback with opportunities for persistence and revision empower teachers? What are the skills of instructional agility? How can teachers process their efforts? How will they know when it worked so they can celebrate? How can they discover the one or two adjustments they can make so they also have the opportunity to try again? How much would teachers' instructional practices improve if they were able to focus on how their instructional agility influences student achievement and confidence? The answers to these questions afford a strong focus for a collaborative team.

These commitments create a space where listening is central—both teachers and students feel that others hear and believe in them. The road to achievement and confidence is paved with time to think, making the complex simple (not easy), an ongoing commitment to co-design, and deliberate practice with targeted feedback.

# Strategies and Tools

In the broader context, the school and district support teachers and teams in developing instructional agility by (1) creating a common definition and rationale of instructional agility, (2) assessing their current reality, (3) developing common protocols and processes, and (4) differentiating professional learning for teachers and teams. To get to this powerful practice, the following strategies help cultivate the broader context where instructional agility takes root.

## Strategy 1: Create a Common Definition and Rationale

Teachers must engage in conversations with colleagues to fully understand the concept of instructional agility and its rationale. A shared understanding of the way instructional agility supports and plays into the work is essential for teachers to meaningfully develop this practice in not only classrooms but in the collective culture of the school.

Being instructionally agile means teachers have the capacity to use emerging evidence to make real-time modifications within the context of the learning they expect. Whether at the classroom or school level, teachers realize the true power of assessment when they use emerging assessment results to determine what comes next in the learning. Table 7.1 (page 156) describes the work of teachers and students in

*Table 7.1: Instructional Agility—What It Is and What It Is Not*

| What It Is | What It Is Not |
|---|---|
| Teachers intentionally use observations, feedback, and questioning in the moment of instruction while students do something with what they are asked to learn. | Student work is permanent rather than fluid, ever changing, and always growing. |
| Teachers act in the moment to respond to student learning needs. | Teachers respond to everything, even outside of the learning target, and get off track. |
| Students are able to identify their strengths and next steps. Instruction helps facilitate this for students when assessment is in action. | Feedback shuts down learning. |
| Instruction mobilizes students to understand that learning is a process. Students collaborate in partnerships with teachers and peers to achieve in their work at expected levels. Students develop and come to value their self-efficacy. | Instruction debilitates students from trying at all or attempting to learn more. A teacher's tone can create a sense of possibility and engagement, or it can make students feel demotivated or paralyzed to take the next step. |

*Visit **go.SolutionTree.com/assessment** for a free reproducible version of this table.*

an instructionally agile environment compared to one that is not. This table may be helpful as teachers and administrators work to create a common definition and understanding of what instructional agility looks like in practice.

Consider engaging in the following.

- Host a book study where groups of teachers take one aspect of instructional agility (questioning, mobilizing, observing, or practicing) and dialogue with colleagues. The end goal is a common definition and a set of strategies that teachers can implement in their classrooms.

- Encourage administrators and other instructional leaders to facilitate discussion around instructional agility. Teachers generate lists of strategies. Each teacher commits to trying a strategy for a few weeks. They come back together to share the impact of those strategies. Use one of the dialogue strategies in chapter 2 (page 29).

- Have administrators and teachers work together to identify what instructional agility is and what it is not (using the resources in this book). Volunteer teachers record lessons on video to create a collection of strategies that teachers can look at and then implement in their classrooms. Teachers watch each other in person or through these videos, discussing the most powerful aspects of instructional agility.

These strategies can help develop a common understanding of instructional agility.

# Strategy 2: Assess Your Current Reality

Once stakeholders define and discuss instructional agility in the broader context (which includes parents and families as well as schools), it is essential to assess the level of understanding and implementation of the broader context of instructional agility and classroom practices. Figure 7.2 displays statements teachers can consider to help them understand how best to support instructional agility in their school. For each statement, individuals, leadership teams, and administration mark a level of implementation. *Unsure* means they have questions about what the statement means or do not have a shared understanding of the concept. *Exploring* means they have had intentional professional learning experiences or conversations that focus on the statement. *Implementing* means they have clear examples of observations or artifacts that show evidence of the statement in action. *Impacting* means there is evidence of that statement increasing student achievement, student confidence, teacher confidence, and teacher effectiveness.

| **Directions:** Mark the following statements to understand your strengths and next steps in developing your instructional agility context. | | | | |
|---|:---:|:---:|:---:|:---:|
| **Task** | Unsure | Exploring | Implementing | Impacting |
| Develop the assessment architecture that focuses student learning.<br>• The school and district facilitate and ensure teachers work in collaboration to do the following.<br>  • Determine the meaning of standards and other expected learning.<br>  • Unpack and repack standards to develop learning progressions.<br>  • Design and plan assessment evidence aligned to standards and learning progressions.<br>  • Analyze assessment evidence to improve the assessment design's accuracy and plan more effective instruction and intervention. | | | | |
| Map standards or learning progressions by unit (school and district supports).<br>• The school and district facilitate and ensure teachers work in collaboration to do the following.<br>  • Identify the series of logical steps required in the learning process of achieving the standards. | | | | |

***Figure 7.2: Taking inventory of instructional agility context and practice.***

continued ➔

| Task | Unsure | Exploring | Implementing | Impacting |
|------|--------|-----------|--------------|-----------|
| • Clarify key points for assessing the standards.<br>• Isolate potential points when and where students might struggle or misunderstand the standards.<br>• Formulate the formative pathway that can help teachers accurately diagnose learning on the way to achieving the standards. | | | | |
| Engineer conversations in the classroom.<br>• Teachers unpack speaking and listening standards and determine characteristics of quality conversations in the context of their grade and content.<br>• Teachers consistently use discussion formats, rules, and roles to get students talking.<br>• Teachers listen to student discussion to interpret how learners are understanding intended standards.<br>• Teachers make instructional maneuvers to deepen students' learning based on their interpretations.<br>• Students are consistently engaged in conversation in all classes and all grade levels. | | | | |
| Use questioning.<br>• Teachers design questions to gather information on standards.<br>• Teachers work on interpreting student responses to questions and then make moves to deepen understanding.<br>• Students ask questions. Teachers structure classroom environments so students ask questions.<br>• Teachers interpret questions and flexibly respond to student understanding in the moment of instruction. | | | | |
| Observe specific concepts.<br>• Teachers focus their observations on essential standards or understandings.<br>• Teacher observations of students' words, actions, and facial expressions lead to instructional maneuvers and feedback that students act on and, in turn, grow from. | | | | |
| Mobilize students to be instructionally agile.<br>Students are intentionally:<br>• Co-constructing criteria with their teachers and peers | | | | |

| | | | | |
|---|---|---|---|---|
| • Using assessment information to self-assess, identifying what they know and what they need to do next<br>• Using assessment information to self-regulate, identifying what shuts them down and what keeps them going<br>• Setting goals toward essential standards and tracking their progress over the course of the year<br>• Engaging in peer assessment | | | | |
| Include lots of practice.<br>• Teachers use homework as information to inform instruction in the moment.<br>• Teachers guide students to use their homework to understand their strengths and next steps in learning. | | | | |
| Examine student work in collaboration.<br>• Teachers collaboratively review student work on essential learning standards to interpret the work and make instructional plans to help students grow. | | | | |
| Analyze common or collaborative formative assessment data.<br>• Teachers determine which students have mastered the learning targets and which need additional time and support. | | | | |
| Consistently review policies and practices at the school and district levels.<br>• Assess the extent to which the following commitments are experienced by teachers and students.<br>  • Teachers and students feel that the school and district believe in them.<br>  • Teachers and students feel they have ample time to think and innovate.<br>  • Teachers co-design learning with students in classrooms, and teachers co-design their professional learning.<br>  • Teachers and students experience feedback practices that increase their confidence and achievement. | | | | |

*Visit **go.SolutionTree.com/assessment** for a free reproducible version of this figure.*

Leaders and teachers may also identify the key characteristics of instructional agility in the classroom and use a rubric or progression to improve the impact of their implementation. Figure 7.3 (page 160) is one example of a progression that could help a system's teachers understand how to develop instructional agility in their classrooms. The figure identifies four specific instructional agility qualities—(1) accuracy, (2) feedback, (3) dialogue and questioning—that teachers can observe and that individuals and teams can reflect on.

| Criteria | Beginning | Growing | Implementing | Impacting |
|---|---|---|---|---|
| **Accuracy** | Teachers focus on activities and may post an agenda of activities. | Teachers describe learning and may post learning targets, or they may simply explain what is to be learned. Activities clearly relate to the learning. | Teachers post learning targets for reference and student reflection. Students can articulate what they are learning. | Teachers post learning targets for reference and student reflection during and after activities. Students track essential learning and can articulate where they are strong as well as next steps for improvement. There is clear evidence that feedback and dialogue impact learning. |
| **Feedback** | Teachers leave feedback, if any, in either written or verbal form for students to figure out and act on. | Teachers offer descriptive feedback in either written or verbal form to individuals or to groups in the class. Feedback clearly provides descriptions and strengths and offers next steps. | Feedback directly relates to learning goals. Students act on that feedback either through revision or dialogue. Students can articulate why they are working on a particular task or revising it. | Students provide each other feedback from a very specific set of criteria or learning targets. Students reflect on that feedback. Students ask questions and generate new ways to understand. |
| **Dialogue and Questioning** | Teachers explain, describe, and present. | Teachers lead discussions, engaging some students who offer comments or questions. | Teachers structure dialogue and questioning so students interact, question, and sustain discussion about the learning targets. | Students generate dialogue and questions, interacting with each other and making connections to the learning targets. Students talk 60 percent of the time. |

**Figure 7.3:** *Instructional agility implementation rubric.*

Visit **go.SolutionTree.com/assessment** *for a free reproducible version of this figure.*

## Strategy 3: Develop Common Protocols and Processes

Develop common protocols and processes at a systems level to ensure accurate interpretations and assessment evidence. The following protocols set the stage for powerful instructional agility practices: (1) unpack and repack standards, (2) determine an assessment plan for gathering accurate information, (3) design assessment items for error analysis, and (4) analyze common errors.

### Unpack and Repack Standards

*Source: Adapted from Vagle, 2015.*

After you have identified learning targets, review them to ensure they represent the standard's essence and adjust accordingly. Consider the following four steps.

1. Circle verbs in the identified standards.

2. Underline concepts, vocabulary, and context that are important.

3. Write learning targets using the verbs circled in the standards (step 1).

    a. Identify what students need to know and be able to do to achieve the standards.

    b. Write the prerequisite learning goals.

    c. Write learning targets that extend and deepen the learning.

4. Organize the learning goals in order of complexity. See figure 7.4 (page 162), which shows an example of learning goals unpacked and placed in cognitive order for a fourth-grade English language arts standard.

### Determine an Assessment Plan for Gathering Accurate Information

The following steps will help you determine an assessment plan.

1. Identify the learning goals. Be sure they represent the simple and more complex learning goals you intended students to learn, that you taught, and that students have mastered.

2. Determine the type of method or item to measure this learning goal (for example, blog, podcast, Socratic seminar, multiple choice, or essay).

3. Identify the number of items for each learning goal (or the percentage of importance). (We recommend four to six items for classroom assessment per learning target on simple and medium complexity targets.)

4. When designing a formative assessment, choose the essential-to-know, hard-to-teach, hard-to-learn goals and design instruction so you can determine student strengths and next steps.

5. When designing a summative assessment, choose standard level and deeper learning targets.

| Learning Target |
| --- |
| I can **evaluate** the effectiveness of a first- or secondhand account. This means I can explain how the viewpoint enhances or distracts from the message of the text.<br>I can create a first- or secondhand account of a situation. |
| I can **compare and contrast** a first- and secondhand account. This means I can analyze how a text is different when told from different perspectives and explain why that is important. |
| I can **describe** the perspective in first- and secondhand accounts. |
| I can **identify** whether a text is a first- or secondhand account.<br>I can **explain** what makes an account first- or secondhand. |

**Figure 7.4:** *Unpacked and repacked standard.*

From the unpacked and repacked standard, accurate interpretations depend on assessment evidence. Figure 7.5 provides an assessment plan for a fourth-grade standard. The first column identifies the learning targets from the standard. The second column describes the items or the percentage of importance. The percentage of importance indicates the learning targets that are most important and require the majority of time. The more important the learning target, the more time learners and teachers work to achieve it. The third column describes the method or type of evidence used to determine levels of proficiency.

| Learning Target | Total Number of Items or Percentage of Importance | Method |
| --- | --- | --- |
| I can **evaluate** the effectiveness of a first- or secondhand account. This means I can explain how the viewpoint enhances or distracts from the message of the text.<br>I can create a first- or secondhand account of a situation. | 40 (beyond standard level, so assessed formatively and summatively) | Essay<br>Editorial<br>Podcast |
| I can **compare and contrast** a first- and secondhand account. This means I can analyze how a text is different when told from different perspectives and explain why that is important. | 20 (at standard level, so assessed formatively and summatively) | Socratic dialogue<br>Graphic organizer |

| I can **describe** the perspective in first- and secondhand accounts. | Only used formatively | Short answer |
|---|---|---|
| I can **identify** whether a text is a first- or secondhand account.<br>I can **explain** what makes an account first- or secondhand. | Only used formatively | Short answer |

**Note:** When you have already designed an assessment, align each item to the learning target in the chart. See how closely your current assessment matches the learning goals for that unit. When doing this, cross out the Method column and insert the item number or task.

***Figure 7.5: Assessment plan.***

## Design Assessment Items for Error Analysis

Teams review the list of learning targets and determine which are essential to know, hard to teach, hard to learn, and require more time (Vagle, 2015). Teams design assessment items to gather evidence on these high-priority learning targets. Based on student responses to these assessment items, teachers interpret what students understand and what they need to work on. Assessments designed to uncover strengths and misconceptions lead to more accurate analysis and interpretation—something essential for instructional agility. Figure 7.6 shows an example of assessment items a team might use to check student understanding on various aspects of a standard.

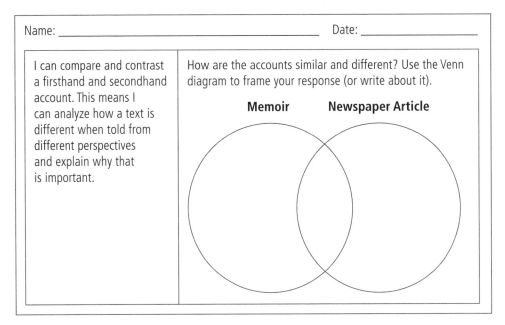

***Figure 7.6: Assessment items.***

continued ➔

| | |
|---|---|
| I can describe the perspective told in firsthand or secondhand accounts. | Both accounts discuss the destruction of schools. From reading both texts, we learn that many students had to attend schools in churches or with students from other districts. |
| | What do we learn from Elizabeth about what it was like to go to school after the hurricane? |
| | What words or phrases in the memoir made you think this? |
| | What do we learn from the newspaper article about what it was like to go to school after the hurricane? |
| | What words or phrases in the newspaper article made you think this? |
| I can identify whether a text is a firsthand or secondhand account. I can explain what makes an account firsthand or secondhand. | Which account is firsthand? Explain why. Which account is secondhand? Explain why. |

## Analyze Common Errors

Next, teams review items from an assessment to understand students' learning strengths and next steps. Based on their interpretations of student work, teachers plan intervention or instructional responses. In other words, they co-plan how to address those needs, designing a lesson to use the next day (or soon thereafter) to meet the learning needs identified in the assessment items. After they employ the lesson they designed, teachers check with students using another brief assessment to see if they have a deeper understanding of what they worked on. Then the team reviews these check-ins to see how effective the interventions were.

Figure 7.7 shows the misconceptions that emerged from analyzing student work, followed by a possible instructional plan or intervention, and the students who need work in that particular area. This graphic organizer helps plan the logistics of targeted instruction.

These protocols and conversations develop teachers' ability to interpret more accurately—recognizing the root cause of students' current state of understanding—and develop innovate lessons that help learners achieve at high levels.

| Next Step: Misconceptions and Enrichment | Possible Interventions | Student Names |
|---|---|---|
| Responses show students understand the texts but don't know the difference between firsthand and secondhand accounts. | Provide another and different example of what firsthand and secondhand accounts are.<br>• Provide direct instruction to point out words that give clues.<br>• Model responses.<br>• All students revise their original responses. | Alyssa<br>Javion<br>Matt<br>Jack<br>Laura<br>Jasmine<br>Maia |
| Responses show students understand the difference between firsthand and secondhand accounts but need more work on explaining why they are different, using parts of the text to support their thinking. | • Give feedback.<br>• Model responses.<br>• All students revise their original responses. | Lisa<br>Xavier<br>Kim<br>Beth<br>Boden<br>Finn<br>Carl<br>Rhys |
| Responses show students understand and demonstrate mastery. | Provide enrichment.<br>• Create a second part of the memoir.<br>• Research another major event. Find a firsthand and secondhand account to share with the class. | Samantha<br>Elise<br>Jamar<br>Christine<br>Jose<br>Tami<br>Chase |

**Figure 7.7:** *Team response to assessment evidence.*

*Visit* **go.SolutionTree.com/assessment** *for a free reproducible version of this figure.*

# Strategy 4: Differentiate Professional Learning

When teachers experience responsive learning environments for their own practice, this sets the tone and provides a model of how to do something different with their students, such as collaborating in open spaces and developing differentiated learning agendas for different teams of teachers.

## Open Spaces

Teachers, in collaboration and individually, reflect on their own work and identify persisting problems, challenges, or new ideas to dig into. As they identify those areas, they post them with a time and a place for discussion and dialogue. This posting provides time and space to problem-solve the challenges and questions that teachers identify.

All of those interested in digging into that conversation or challenge attend. The place may be a physical location or a virtual meeting. Most often, the person posing the challenge attends that session and facilitates the conversation, but does not make a presentation. The group documents its insights either electronically or on paper. At the end of the open space session, each individual and team commits to some kind of action to improve or transform their practice. Within a few weeks, the staff meet or check in to revisit the impact of these new ideas or solutions. Voice and choice are central to this differentiation. Teachers voice the areas they want to learn more about and then choose how they will spend their time. Figure 7.8 provides an example of what this could be like.

| Time | Question or Challenge | Location | Key Insights (Shared Post Session) |
|------|----------------------|----------|-------------------------------------|
| 10:00 a.m. | How do we use observations in mathematics and science to give students feedback efficiently and effectively (so they act on it)? This leads to wondering how we manage having many things happening at the same time in our classrooms. We aim to develop some solutions that help us identify practical ways to give feedback when all students need something different. | Room 201 | |
| 10:15 a.m.–12:15 p.m. | What are key elements of questions that give us better information regarding student understanding on essential learning targets? Look at this and then develop questions. | Room 204 | |
| 1:15 p.m.–3:15 p.m. | How do we teach and guide students to track their learning on essential standards? | Room 210 | |

**Figure 7.8: *Open spaces—professional learning and dialogue.***
*Visit **go.SolutionTree.com/assessment** for a free reproducible version of this figure.*

However, it is absolutely essential that everyone understands the components of the work so challenges and innovations are in the context of helping all students achieve at higher levels and gain confidence, not just solving problems (such as being late to class or not doing homework) that may be a symptom of a different root cause.

### Differentiated Learning Agendas

Leadership teams pose the framework, which may be a common definition of instructional agility and accompanying practices. Figure 7.2 (page 157) is an example of a framework that indicates what teacher teams are doing in various aspects of the work. Teacher teams assess their progress and then develop an agenda for the day that includes an outcome they will share at the day's end. Small sessions throughout provide support and learning on topics that are new or training that is necessary to move their work forward. Typically, the principal and instructional coaches collaborate with department chairs or grade level leads to develop these sessions.

# Conclusion

You can give teachers strategies, but when you give them a process and a rationale, the impact is authentic teacher investment; it is the move from compliance to commitment. When teachers create and design assessments both individually and together based on reflection of their own practice, they build a collective sense of investment in helping students learn. Leaders help teachers develop a process for thinking about how students learn, interpreting assessment results, and planning for how to help students continue to learn. This process, supported by professional training and protected time to focus and collaborate, builds a natural, ongoing expectation of instructional agility. It is through instructional agility that educators build relationships with students in ways that send students the message that their learning is of utmost importance and that the adults in their lives will do anything to ensure they achieve.

# Pause and Ponder

Take a few moments to reflect on the following questions.

- Describe how the broader context, such as the school or district, can be instructionally agile.
- What kind of culture must we develop in order to do this? What are the four commitments that contribute to influencing a culture in which instructional agility can thrive?
- Use figure 7.2 (page 157) and figure 7.3 (page 160) to assess your system's strengths and next steps.

- What routines, protocols, or processes are in place in your school to create instructionally agile learning environments? In what ways could you enhance these routines, protocols, or processes to create an even stronger relationship between assessment results and real-time instructional maneuvers?

- In what ways have you and your colleagues already differentiated your professional learning experiences? In what ways could you enhance professional learning differentiation?

# APPENDIX
# INSTRUCTIONAL AGILITY MANIFESTO

*Visit **go.SolutionTree.com/assessment** for a free reproducible version of this appendix.*

As educators, we commit to the following principles.

- Our highest priority is to support learning through engendering hope, building efficacy, and increasing achievement for our students.

- We recognize education to be the great equalizer and, as such, we commit to guaranteeing high levels of success for each and every student entrusted to our care.

- We pledge to remain instructionally agile at all times, responding to the emerging evidence as we are teaching in precise yet flexible ways.

Through our instruction, we commit to the following.

- We will care deeply but never justify or accept less from our students.

- We will empower but never abandon our students to their own devices.

- We will obligate excellence but never impose rigidity.

- We will challenge thinking but never spur angst.

- We will ignite passion but never inflame indignation.

To accomplish our goal, we will work collaboratively to do the following.

- Solve complex challenges.

- Explore best practice research.

- Engage in our own action research.

- Share instructional strategies.

- Attend to quality designs and technical excellence.

- Question our results while reflecting on our effectiveness.

- Commit to continual improvement.

We understand that it is impossible to perfect the work of teaching, yet we accept the moral imperative to never stop trying.

# REFERENCES & RESOURCES

Allen, J. D., & Dai, Y. (2016, April). *A comparative analysis using reciprocal questioning with college students in China and the United States.* Paper presented at the annual meeting of the American Educational Research Association, Washington, DC.

Andrade, H. L. (2010). Students as the definitive source of formative assessment: Academic self-assessment and the self-regulation of learning. In H. L. Andrade & G. J. Cizek (Eds.), *Handbook of formative assessment* (pp. 90–105). New York: Routledge.

Andrade, H. L. (2013). Classroom assessment in the context of learning theory and research. In J. H. McMillan (Ed.), *SAGE handbook of research on classroom assessment* (pp. 17–34). Thousand Oaks, CA: SAGE.

Andrade, H. L., Du, Y., & Mycek, K. (2010). Rubric-referenced self-assessment and middle school students' writing. *Assessment in Education: Principles, Policy & Practice, 17*(2), 199–214.

Applebee, A. N., Langer, J. A., Nystrand, M., & Gamoran, A. (2003). Discussion-based approaches to developing understanding: Classroom instruction and student performance in middle and high school English. *American Educational Research Journal, 40*(3), 685–730.

Atkinson, P. (2003). *Assessment 5–14: What do pupils and parents think?* Glasgow, Scotland: University of Glasgow. (ERIC Document Reproduction Service No. ED480897)

Bennett, S., & Kalish, N. (2006). *The case against homework: How homework is hurting our children and what we can do about it.* New York: Crown.

Berger, W. (2014). *A more beautiful question: The power of inquiry to spark breakthrough ideas.* New York: Bloomsbury.

Black, P. (2013). Formative and summative aspects of assessment: Theoretical and research foundations in the context of pedagogy. In J. H. McMillan (Ed.), *SAGE handbook of research on classroom assessment* (pp. 167–195). Thousand Oaks, CA: SAGE.

Black, P., & Wiliam, D. (1998). Inside the black box: Raising standards through classroom assessment. *Phi Delta Kappan, 80*(2), 139–144.

Blanchard, K. (2015). *Feedback is the breakfast of champions.* Accessed at https://howwelead .org/2015/01/07/feedback-is-the-breakfast-of-champions-2/ on September 18, 2017.

Brookhart, S. M. (2007). Expanding views about formative classroom assessment: A review of the literature. In J. H. McMillan (Ed.), *Formative classroom assessment: Theory into practice* (pp. 43–62). New York: Teachers College Press.

Brookhart, S. M. (2013a). Classroom assessment in the context of motivation theory and research. In J. H. McMillan (Ed.), *SAGE handbook of research on classroom assessment* (pp. 35–54). Thousand Oaks, CA: SAGE.

Brookhart, S. (2013b). Grading. In J. McMillan (Ed.), *SAGE handbook of research on classroom assessment* (pp. 257–271). Thousand Oaks, CA: SAGE.

Brookhart, S. M., Andolina, M., Zuza, M., & Furman, R. (2004). Minute math: An action research study of student self-assessment. *Educational Studies in Mathematics, 57*(2), 213–227.

Brown, G. T. L., & Harris, L. R. (2013). Student self-assessment. In J. H. McMillan (Ed.), *SAGE handbook of research on classroom assessment* (pp. 367–393). Thousand Oaks, CA: SAGE.

Brown, N. J. S., & Wilson, M. (2011). A model of cognition: The missing cornerstone of assessment. *Educational Psychology Review, 23*(2), 221–234.

Brown Wessling, S. (n.d.). *Pinwheel discussions: Texts in conversation* [Video]. Accessed at www.teachingchannel.org/videos/high-school-literature-lesson-plan on March 26, 2014.

Bryant, D., & Carless, D. (2010). Peer assessment in a test-dominated setting: Empowering, boring or facilitating examination preparation? *Educational Research for Policy and Practice, 9*(1), 3–15.

Butler, D., & Winne, P. (1995). Feedback and self-regulated learning: A theoretical synthesis. *Review of Educational Research, 65*(3), 245–281.

Butler, R. (1988). Enhancing and undermining intrinsic motivation: The effects of task-involving and ego-involving evaluation on interest and performance. *British Journal of Educational Psychology, 58*(1), 1–14.

Campbell, C. (2013). Research on teacher competency in classroom assessment. In J. H. McMillan (Ed.), *SAGE handbook of research on classroom assessment* (pp. 71–84). Thousand Oaks, CA: SAGE.

Campbell, C., & Evans, J. A. (2000). Investigation of preservice teachers' classroom assessment practices during student teaching. *Journal of Educational Research, 93*(6), 350–355.

Canadian Council on Learning. (2009). *Lessons in learning: Homework helps, but not always.* Ottawa, Ontario, Canada: Author.

Chapin, S., O'Conner, C., & Anderson, N. (2013). *Classroom discussions in math: A teacher's guide for using talk moves to support the Common Core and more* (3rd ed.). Sausalito, CA: Math Solutions.

Chappuis, J. (2014). *Seven strategies of assessment for learning* (2nd ed.). Boston: Pearson.

Charteris, J., & Smardon, D. (2015). Teacher agency and dialogic feedback: Using classroom data for practitioner inquiry. *Teaching and Teacher Education, 50*, 114–123.

Cizek, G. J. (2000). Pockets of resistance in the assessment revolution. *Educational Measurement: Issues and Practice, 19*(2), 16–23, 33.

Cizek, G. J. (2009). Reliability and validity of information about student achievement: Comparing large-scale and classroom testing contexts. *Theory Into Practice, 48*(1), 63–71.

Cooper, H., Robinson, J. C., & Patall, E. A. (2006). Does homework improve academic achievement? A synthesis of research, 1987–2003. *Review of Educational Research, 76*(1), 1–62.

Daft, M. (2008, February 13). Artists as education consultants. *Education Week, 27*(23), 32–33.

Davies, A. (2007). Involving students in the classroom assessment process. In D. Reeves (Ed.), *Ahead of the curve: The power of assessment to transform teaching and learning* (pp. 31–57). Bloomington, IN: Solution Tree Press.

Depka, E. (2015). *Bringing homework into focus: Tools and tips to enhance practices, design, and feedback.* Bloomington, IN: Solution Tree Press.

Dougherty, E. (2012). *Assignments matter: Making the connections that help students meet standards.* Alexandria, VA: Association for Supervision and Curriculum Development.

DuFour, R., DuFour, R., & Eaker, R. (2008). *Revisiting Professional Learning Communities at Work: New insights for improving schools.* Bloomington, IN: Solution Tree Press.

DuFour, R., DuFour, R., Eaker, R., Many, T. W., & Mattos, M. (2016). *Learning by doing: A handbook for professional learning communities at work* (3rd ed.). Bloomington, IN: Solution Tree Press.

Dunning, D., Heath, C., & Suls, J. M. (2004). Flawed self-assessment: Implications for health, education, and the workplace. *Psychological Science in the Public Interest, 5*(3), 69–106.

Dweck, C. (2006). *Mindset: The new psychology of success.* New York: Random House.

Eren, O., & Henderson, D. J. (2008). The impact of homework on student achievement. *Econometrics Journal, 11*(2), 326–348.

Ericsson, K. A., Krampe, R. T., & Tesch-Römer, C. (1993). The role of deliberate practice in the acquisition of expert performance. *Psychological Review, 100*(3), 363–406.

Erkens, C. (2013, October 21). *Data notebooks* [Blog post]. Accessed at http://anamcaraconsulting.com/wordpress/2013/10/21/data-notebooks on October 21, 2013.

Erkens, C. (2014, May 30). *The power of homework as a formative tool* [Blog post]. Accessed at http://anamcaraconsulting.com/wordpress/2014/05/30/the-power-of-homework-as-a-formative-tool on May 30, 2014.

Erkens, C. (2015, April 21). *Groupings for collaborative learning* [Blog post]. Accessed at www.solutiontree.com/blog/?s=groupings on March 27, 2017.

Erkens, C. (2016). *Collaborative common assessments: Teamwork. Instruction. Results.* Bloomington, IN: Solution Tree Press.

Erkens, C., Schimmer, T., & Vagle, N. D. (2017). *Essential assessment: Six tenets for bringing hope, efficacy, and achievement to the classroom.* Bloomington, IN: Solution Tree Press.

Fail often, fail well. (2011, April 14). *The Economist.* Accessed at www.economist.com /node/18557776 on March 27, 2017.

Finn, J. D., & Zimmer, K. S. (2012). Student engagement: What is it? Why does it matter? In S. L. Christenson, A. L. Reschly, & C. Wylie (Eds.), *Handbook of research on student engagement* (pp. 97–131). New York: Springer.

Fisher D., & Frey, N. (2007). *Checking for understanding: Formative assessment techniques for your classroom.* Alexandria, VA: Association for Supervision and Curriculum Development.

Fisher, D., & Frey, N. (2010). *Guided instruction: How to develop confident and successful students.* Alexandria, VA: Association for Supervision and Curriculum Development.

Fisher, D., & Frey, N. (2012). Feedback for learning. *Educational Leadership, 70*(1), 42–46.

Fisher, D., & Frey, N. (2015). *Unstoppable learning: Seven essential elements to unleash student potential.* Bloomington, IN: Solution Tree Press.

Fisher, D., Frey, N., & Pumpian, I. (2012). *How to create a culture of achievement in your school and classroom.* Alexandria, VA: Association for Supervision and Curriculum Development.

Ford, H., & Crowther, S. (1922). *My life and work.* New York: Doubleday.

Frey, N., Fisher, D., & Everlove, S. (2009). *Productive group work: How to engage students, build teamwork, and promote understanding.* Alexandria, VA: Association for Supervision and Curriculum Development.

Gawande, A. (2010). *The checklist manifesto: How to get things right.* New York: Metropolitan Books.

Gill, B., & Schlossman, S. L. (2004). Villain or savior? The American discourse on homework, 1850–2003. *Theory Into Practice, 43*(3), 174–181.

GLOBE Program. (n.d.). *For teachers.* Accessed at www.globe.gov/do-globe/for-teachers on March 28, 2017.

Gregory, K., Cameron, C., & Davies, A. (1997). *Knowing what counts: Setting and using criteria.* Courtenay, British Columbia, Canada: Connections.

Guskey, T. R. (2015). *On your mark: Challenging the conventions of grading and reporting.* Bloomington, IN: Solution Tree Press.

Hambrick, D. Z., Oswald, F. L., Altmann, E. M., Meinz, E. J., Gobet, F., & Campitelli, G. (2013). Deliberate practice: Is that all it takes to become an expert? *Intelligence, 45*(1), 34–45.

Hattie, J. (2009). *Visible learning: A synthesis of over 800 meta-analyses relating to achievement.* London: Routledge.

Hattie, J. (2012). *Visible learning for teachers: Maximizing impact on learning.* London: Routledge.

Hattie, J., & Timperley, H. (2007). The power of feedback. *Review of Educational Research, 77*(1), 81–112.

Hattie, J., & Yates, G. (2014). *Visible learning and the science of how we learn.* London: Routledge.

Heritage, M. (2010). *Formative assessment: Making it happen in the classroom.* Thousand Oaks, CA: Corwin Press.

Heritage, M. (2013). Gathering evidence of student understanding. In J. H. McMillan (Ed.), *SAGE handbook of research on classroom assessment* (pp. 179–195). Thousand Oaks, CA: SAGE.

Heritage, M. (2016, April). *The use of formative assessment results to educate all in diverse democracies: Research results from four different countries.* Presented at the annual meeting of the American Educational Research Association, Washington, DC.

Horn, M. B., & Staker, H. (2015). *Blended: Using disruptive innovation to improve schools.* San Francisco: Jossey-Bass.

Kane, M. T. (2006). Validation. In R. L. Brennan (Ed.), *Educational measurement* (4th ed., pp. 17–64). Washington, DC: National Council on Measurement in Education.

Kay, K., & Greenhill, V. (2013). *The leader's guide to 21st century education: 7 steps for schools and districts.* Boston: Pearson.

Keller, B. (2007, September 19). No easy project. *Education Week, 27*(4), 21–23.

Kelly, S., & Price, H. (2014). Changing patterns of engagement in the transition to high school. In D. J. Shernoff & J. Bempechat (Eds.), *Engaging youth in schools: Evidence-based models to guide future innovations* (pp. 15–36). New York: Teachers College Press.

King, A. (1990). Enhancing peer interaction and learning in the classroom through reciprocal questioning. *American Educational Research Journal, 27*(4), 664–687.

King, A. (2002). Structuring peer interaction to promote high-level cognitive processing. *Theory Into Practice, 41*(1), 3–39.

Klem, A. M., & Connell, J. P. (2004). Relationships matter: Linking teacher support to student engagement and achievement. *Journal of School Health, 74*(7), 262–273.

Kluger, A. N., & DeNisi, A. (1996). The effects of feedback interventions on performance: A historical review, a meta-analysis, and a preliminary feedback intervention theory. *Psychological Bulletin, 119*(2), 254–284.

Knight, J. (2007). *Instructional coaching: A partnership approach to improving instruction.* Thousand Oaks, CA: Corwin Press.

Knight, J. (2014). *Focus on teaching: Using video for high-impact instruction.* Thousand Oaks, CA: Corwin Press.

Kohn, A. (2006). *The homework myth: Why our kids get too much of a bad thing.* Cambridge, MA: Da Capo Press.

Lane, S. (2010). *Performance assessment: The state of the art.* Stanford, CA: Stanford Center for Opportunity Policy in Education.

Lane, S. (2013). Performance assessment. In J. H. McMillan (Ed.), *SAGE handbook of research on classroom assessment* (pp. 313–329). Thousand Oaks, CA: SAGE.

Lemov, D., Woolway, E., & Yezzi, K. (2012). *Practice perfect: 42 rules for getting better at getting better.* San Francisco: Jossey-Bass.

Louis, K. S., Leithwood, K., Wahlstrom, K. L., & Anderson, S. E. (2010). *Learning from leadership: Investigating the links to improved student learning.* Minneapolis: University of Minnesota, Center for Applied Research and Educational Improvement. Accessed at www.wallacefoundation.org/knowledge-center/Documents/Investigating-the-Links-to -Improved-Student-Learning.pdf on March 27, 2016.

Marzano, R. J. (2007). *The art and science of teaching: A comprehensive framework for effective instruction.* Alexandria, VA: Association for Supervision and Curriculum Development.

Marzano, R. J., & Pickering, D. J. (2007a). The case for and against homework. *Educational Leadership, 64*(6), 74–79.

Marzano, R. J., & Pickering, D. J. (2007b). Errors and allegations about research on homework. *Phi Delta Kappan, 88*(7), 507–513.

Marzano, R. J., Pickering, D. J., & Pollock, J. E. (2001). *Classroom instruction that works: Research-based strategies for increasing student achievement.* Alexandria, VA: Association for Supervision and Curriculum Development.

Mehrabian, A. (1981). *Silent messages: Implicit communication of emotions and attitudes* (2nd ed.). Belmont, CA: Wadsworth.

Messick, S. (1994). The interplay of evidence and consequences in the validation of performance assessments. *Educational Researcher, 23*(1), 13–24.

Mislevy, R. J., Steinberg, L. S., & Almond, R. G. (2003). On the structure of educational assessments. *Measurement: Interdisciplinary Research and Perspectives, 1*(1), 3–62.

Munns, G., & Woodward, H. (2006). Student engagement and student self-assessment: The REAL framework. *Assessment in Education: Principles, Policy & Practice, 13*(2), 193–213.

National Council of Teachers of Mathematics. (n.d.) *Executive summary: Principles and standards for school mathematics.* Accessed at www.nctm.org/uploadedFiles/Standards _and_Positions/PSSM_ExecutiveSummary.pdf on October 28, 2016.

National Education Association. (n.d.). *Preparing 21st century students for a global society: An educator's guide to the "four Cs."* Accessed at www.nea.org/assets/docs/A-Guide-to -Four-Cs.pdf on March 14, 2014.

National Governors Association Center for Best Practices & Council of Chief State School Officers. (2010). *Common Core State Standards for English language arts and literacy in history/social studies, science, and technical subjects.* Washington, DC: Authors. Accessed at www.corestandards.org/assets/CCSSI_ELA%20Standards.pdf on February 15, 2016.

Newmann, F. M., Carmichael, D., & King, M. B. (2016). *Authentic intellectual work: Improving teaching for rigorous learning.* Thousand Oaks, CA: Corwin Press.

Next Generation Science Standards. (2013). *Fourth grade.* Accessed at www.nextgenscience .org/sites/default/files/4%20combined%20DCI%20standards%206.13.13.pdf on October 7, 2016.

Nystrand, M., & Gamoran, A. (1991). Instructional discourse, student engagement, and literature achievement. *Research in the Teaching of English, 25*(3), 261–290.

O'Connor, K. (2009). *How to grade for learning, K–12* (3rd ed.). Thousand Oaks, CA: Corwin Press.

O'Connor, K. (2011). *A repair kit for grading: 15 fixes for broken grades* (2nd ed.). Boston: Pearson.

O'Neill, O. (2002). *A question of trust: The BBC Reith Lectures*. Cambridge, England: Cambridge University Press.

Partnership for 21st Century Skills. (2011). *Framework for 21st century learning*. Accessed at www.p21.org/storage/documents/1.__p21_framework_2-pager.pdf on September 18, 2017.

Pink, D. H. (2009). *Drive: The surprising truth about what motivates us*. New York: Riverhead Books.

Pintrich, P. R., & Zusho, A. (2002). The development of academic self-regulation: The role of cognitive and motivational factors. In A. Wigfield & J. S. Eccles (Eds.), *Development of achievement motivation* (pp. 249–284). San Diego, CA: Academic Press.

Popham, J. (2008). *Transformative assessment in action: An inside look at applying the process*. Alexandria, VA: Association for Supervision and Curriculum Development.

Quote Investigator. (n.d.). *I feel that I am making daily progress*. Accessed at http://quoteinvestigator.com/2014/02/12/casals-progress/ on March 28, 2017.

Quotery. (n.d.). *Michael Jordan*. Accessed at www.quotery.com/quotes/ive-missed-more-than-9000-shots-in-my-career-ive on November 1, 2016.

Ramdass, D., & Zimmerman, B. J. (2008). Effects of self-correction strategy training on middle school students' self-efficacy, self-evaluation, and mathematics division learning. *Journal of Advanced Academics, 20*(1), 18–41.

Reeves, D. (2016). *Elements of grading: A guide to effective practice* (2nd ed.). Bloomington, IN: Solution Tree Press.

Ritchhart, R. (2015). *Creating cultures of thinking: The 8 forces we must master to truly transform our schools*. San Francisco: Jossey-Bass.

Richardson, B. G. (2004). *Career comeback: 8 steps to getting back on your feet when you're fired, laid off, or your business venture has failed—and finding more job satisfaction than ever before*. New York: Broadway Books.

Ruiz-Primo, M. A., & Furtak, E. M. (2006). Informal formative assessment and scientific inquiry: Exploring teachers' practices and student learning. *Educational Assessment, 11*(3–4), 205–235.

Ruiz-Primo, M. A., & Furtak, E. M. (2007). Exploring teachers' informal formative assessment practices and students' understanding in the context of scientific inquiry. *Journal of Educational Research in Science Teaching, 44*(1), 57–84.

Ruiz-Primo, M. A., & Li, M. (2011, April). *Looking into the teachers' feedback practices: How teachers interpret students' work*. Paper presented at the annual meeting of the American Educational Research Association, New Orleans, LA.

Ruiz-Primo, M. A., & Li, M. (2013). Examining formative feedback in the classroom context: New research perspectives. In J. H. McMillan (Ed.), *SAGE handbook of research on classroom assessment* (pp. 215–232). Thousand Oaks, CA: SAGE.

Rumsey, C., & Langrall, C. W. (2016). Promoting mathematical argumentation. *Teaching Children Mathematics, 22*(7), 412–419.

Ryan, R. M., & Deci, E. L. (2000). Self-determination theory and the facilitation of intrinsic motivation, social development, and well-being. *American Psychologist, 55*(1), 68–78.

Saavedra, R., & Kwun, S. K. (1993). Peer evaluation in self-managing work groups. *Journal of Applied Psychology, 78*(3), 450–462.

Sadler, D. R. (1989). Formative assessment and the design of instructional systems. *Instructional Science, 18*(2), 119–144.

Scharber, C., Lewis, C., Psycher, T., & Isaacson, K. (2016). Pathways for all: Teens, tech, and learning. In L. R. Miller, D. Becker, & K. Becker (Eds.), *Technology for transformation: Perspectives of hope in the digital age* (pp. 195–214). Charlotte, NC: Information Age.

Schimmer, T. (2016). *Grading from the inside out: Bringing accuracy to student assessment through a standards-based mindset.* Bloomington, IN: Solution Tree Press.

Schimmer, T., Hillman, G., & Stalets, A. (in press). *Standards-based learning in action: Moving from theory to practice.* Bloomington, IN: Solution Tree Press.

Schulte, M. (2009). *Making a difference.* Unpublished manuscript.

Shepard, L., Hammerness, K., Darling-Hammond, L., Rust, F., Snowden, J. B., Gordon, E., et al. (2005). Assessment. In L. Darling-Hammond & J. Bransford (Eds.), *Preparing teachers for a changing world: What teachers should learn and be able to do* (pp. 275–326). San Francisco: Jossey-Bass.

Shernoff, D. J. (2013). *Optimal learning environments to promote student engagement.* New York: Springer.

Skinner, E. A. & Pitzer, J. R. (2012). Developmental dynamics of student engagement, coping, and everyday resilience. In S. L. Christenson, A. L. Reschly, & C. Wiley (Eds.), *Handbook of research on student engagement* (pp. 131–145). New York: Routledge.

Sladkey, D. (2016, September 30). *Ask me a question* [Blog post]. Accessed at http://teachhighschoolmath.blogspot.com/2016/09/ask-me-question.html on October 5, 2016.

Slavin, R. E., Hurley, E. A., & Chamberlain, A. (2003). Cooperative learning and achievement. In I. B. Weiner (Ed.), *Handbook of psychology* (pp. 177–198). Hoboken, NJ: Wiley.

Stiggins, R. (2008). *An introduction to student-involved assessment* for *learning* (5th ed.). Upper Saddle River, NJ: Pearson.

Tapscott, D. (2013, June 7). The spirit of collaboration is touching all of our lives. *Globe and Mail.* Accessed at www.theglobeandmail.com/opinion/the-spirit-of-collaboration-is-touching-all-of-our-lives/article12409331/ on October 11, 2016.

Tomlinson, C. A., & Moon, T. R. (2013). Differentiation and classroom assessment. In J. H. McMillan (Ed.), *SAGE handbook of research on classroom assessment* (pp. 415–430). Thousand Oaks, CA: SAGE.

Topping, K. J. (2013). Peers as a source of formative and summative assessment. In J. H. McMillan (Ed.), *SAGE handbook of research on classroom assessment* (pp. 395–412). Thousand Oaks, CA: SAGE.

Vagle, N. D. (2014, July). *Foundations of assessment design: Grades 4–8.* Presented at Foundations of Assessment Design, Albuquerque, New Mexico. Accessed at http://newmexicocommoncore.org/uploads/downloads/foundations-of-assessment-design-grades-4-8-14eaecde70.pdf on August 17, 2017.

Vagle, N. D. (2015). *Design in five: Essential phases to create engaging assessment practice.* Bloomington, IN: Solution Tree Press.

van Gennip, N. A. E., Segers, M. S. R., & Tillema, H. H. (2009). Peer assessment for learning from a social perspective: The influence of interpersonal variables and structural features. *Educational Research Review, 4*(1), 41–54.

van Zundert, M., Sluijsmans, D., & van Merrienboer, J. (2010). Effective peer assessment processes: Research findings and future directions. *Learning and Instruction, 20*(4), 270–279.

Vatterott, C. (2009). *Rethinking homework: Best practices that support diverse needs.* Alexandria, VA: Association for Supervision and Curriculum Development.

Weaver, M. E. (1995). Using peer response in the classroom: Students' perspectives. *Research and Teaching in Developmental Education, 12*(1), 31–37.

Weiner, B. (1979). A theory of motivation for some classroom experiences. *Journal of Educational Psychology, 71*(1), 3–25.

Wessling, S. (2014). *Pinwheel discussions: Texts in conversation.* Accessed at www.teachingchannel.org/videos/high-school-literature-lesson-plan on March 26, 2014.

Wiggins, G. (2013, February 12). *Autonomy and the need to back off by design as teachers* [Blog post]. Accessed at https://grantwiggins.wordpress.com/2013/02/12/autonomy-and-the-need-to-back-off-by-design-as-teachers/ on November 27, 2016.

Wiliam, D. (2011). *Embedded formative assessment.* Bloomington, IN: Solution Tree Press.

Wiliam, D. (2015). Designing great hinge questions. *Educational Leadership, 73*(1), 40–44.

Willis, J., & Adie, L. E. (2016, April). *Developing teacher formative assessment practices through professional dialogue: Case studies of practice from Queensland, Australia.* Presented at the annual meeting of the American Educational Research Association, Washington, DC.

Wolfe, P. (2010). *Brain matters: Translating research into classroom practice* (2nd ed.). Alexandria, VA: Association for Supervision and Curriculum Development.

Zhu, P. (2016). *Digital valley: Five pearls of wisdom to make profound influence.* Pennsauken, NJ: BookBaby.

Zimmerman, B. J. (2002). Becoming a self-regulated student: An overview. *Theory Into Practice, 41*(2), 64–70.

Zimmerman, B. J. (2011). Motivational sources and outcomes of self-regulated learning. In B. J. Zimmerman & D. H. Schunk (Eds.), *Handbook of self-regulation of learning and performance* (pp. 49–64). New York: Routledge.

Zimmerman, B. J., & Schunk, D. H. (2011). Self-regulated learning and performance: An introduction and overview. In B. J. Zimmerman & D. H. Schunk (Eds.), *Handbook of self-regulation of learning and performance* (pp. 1–12). New York: Routledge.

# INDEX

### Essential Assessment
*Cassandra Erkens, Tom Schimmer, and Nicole Dimich Vagle*
Discover how to use the power of assessment to instill hope, efficacy, and achievement in your students. Explore six essential tenets of assessment that will help deepen your understanding of assessment to not only meet standards but also enhance students' academic success.
**BKF752**

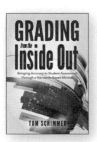

### Grading From the Inside Out
*Tom Schimmer*
The time for grading reform is now. While the transition to standards-based practices may be challenging, it is essential for effective instruction and assessment. Discover the steps your team can take to transform grading and reporting schoolwide.
**BKF646**

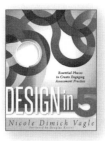

### Design in Five
*Nicole Dimich Vagle*
Discover how to work with your school team to create innovative, effective, engaging assessments using a five-phase design protocol. Explore various types of assessments, learn the traits of quality assessment, and evaluate whether your current assessments meet the design criteria.
**BKF604**

### Collaborative Common Assessments
*Cassandra Erkens*
*Foreword by Richard DuFour*
Reignite the passion and energy assessment practices bring as tools to guide teaching and learning. Strengthen instruction with collaborative common assessments that collect vital information. Explore the practical steps teams must take to establish assessment systems, and discover how to continually improve results.
**BKF605**

## Solution Tree | Press
a division of
Solution Tree

Visit SolutionTree.com or call 800.733.6786 to order.

# "Excellent engagement
in what truly matters
in **assessment**.

# Great examples!"

—Carol Johnson, superintendent,
Central Dauphin School District, Pennsylvania

 PD Services

Our experts draw from decades of research and their own experiences to bring you
practical strategies for designing and implementing quality assessments. You can choose
from a range of customizable services, from a one-day overview to a multiyear process.

## Book your assessment PD today!
**888.763.9045**

Solution Tree